3rd Workshop on Speech and Language Processing for Assistive Technologies 2012

Held at the 2012 Conference of the North American Chapter of the Association for Computational Linguistics: Human Language Technologies (NAACL-HLT 2012)

Montreal, Quebec, Canada
3 – 8 June 2012

ISBN: 978-1-62276-575-1

Printed from e-media with permission by:

Curran Associates, Inc.
57 Morehouse Lane
Red Hook, NY 12571

Printed by Curran Associates, Inc. (2013)

Association for Computational Linguistics
209 N. Eighth Street
Stroudsburg, Pennsylvania 18360

Phone: 1-570-476-8006
Fax: 1-570-476-0860

acl@aclweb.org

Additional copies of this publication are available from:

Curran Associates, Inc.
57 Morehouse Lane
Red Hook, NY 12571 USA
Phone: 845-758-0400
Fax: 845-758-2634
Email: curran@proceedings.com
Web: www.proceedings.com

Introduction

We are pleased to bring you the Proceedings of the Third Workshop on Speech and Language Processing for Assistive Technologies (SLPAT), held in Montreal, Canada on the 7th and 8th of June, 2012. We received 13 paper submissions, of which 8 were chosen for oral presentation and another 2 for demonstration presentation — all 10 papers are included in this volume.

This workshop was intended to bring researchers from all areas of speech and language technology with a common interest in making everyday life more accessible for people with physical, cognitive, sensory, emotional or developmental disabilities. This workshop builds on two previous such workshops (co-located with NAACL HLT 2010 & EMNLP in 2011); it provides an opportunity for individuals from research communities, and the individuals with whom they are working, to share research findings, and to discuss present and future challenges and the potential for collaboration and progress.

While Augmentative and Alternative Communication (AAC) is a particularly apt application area for speech and Natural Language Processing (NLP) technologies, we purposefully made the scope of the workshop broad enough to include assistive technologies (AT) as a whole, even those falling outside of AAC. While we encouraged work that validates methods with human experimental trials, we also accepted work on basic-level innovations and philosophy, inspired by AT/AAC related problems. Thus we have aimed at broad inclusivity, which is also manifest in the diversity of our Program Committee.

We would also like to thank the members of the Program Committee for completing their reviews promptly, and for providing useful feedback for deciding on the program and preparing the final versions of the papers. Thanks also to the NACL organizers for guidance and support. Finally, thanks to the authors of the papers, for submitting such interesting and diverse work, and to the presenters of demos and commercial exhibitions.

Jan Alexandersson, Peter Ljunglöf, Kathy McCoy, Brian Roark and Annalu Waller

Co-organizers of the workshop

Organizers:

Jan Alexandersson, DFKI GmbH
Peter Ljunglöf, University of Gothenburg and Chalmers University of Technology
Kathleen F. McCoy, University of Delaware
Brian Roark, Oregon Health & Science University
Annalu Waller, University of Dundee

Program Committee:

John Arnott, University of Dundee
Melanie Baljko, York University, Canada
Jan Bedrosian, Western Michigan University
Rolf Black, University of Dundee
Torbjørg Breivik, the Language Council of Norway
Tim Bunnell, University of Delaware
Rob Clark, University of Edinburgh
Ann Copestake, University of Cambridge
Stuart Cunningham, University of Sheffield
Rickard Domeij, Stockholm, University
Alistair D.N. Edwards, University of York
Michael Elhadad, Ben-Gurion University
Björn Granström, Royal Institute of Technology, Stockholm
Phil Green, Sheffield University
Mark Hasegawa-Johnson, University of Illinois
Per-Olof Hedvall, Lund University
Jeff Higginbotham, University of Buffalo
Graeme Hirst, University of Toronto
Linda Hoag, Kansas State University
Harry Howard, Tulane University
Matt Huenerfauth, CUNY
Sofie Johansson Kokkinakis, University of Gothenburg
Simon Judge, Barnsley NHS & Sheffield University
Simon King, University of Edinburgh
Per Ola Kristensson, University of St. Andrews
Greg Lesher, Dynavox Technologies, Inc.
Ornella Mich, Foundazione Bruno Kessler
Yael Netzer, Ben-Gurion University
Torbjørn Nordgård, Lingit A/S, Norway
Rupal Patel, Northeastern University
Ehud Reiter, University of Aberdeen

Frank Rudzicz, University of Toronto
Bitte Rydeman, Lund University
Horacio Saggion, Universitat Pompeu Fabra
Howard Shane, Children's Hospital Boston
Fraser Shein, Quillsoft Ltd., Toronto
Kumiko Tanaka-Ishii, University of Tokyo
Nava Tintarev, University of Aberdeen
Keith Vertanen, Montana Tech of The University of Montana
Tonio Wandmacher, SYSTRAN, Paris, France
Jan-Oliver Wülfing, Fraunhofer Centre Birlinghoven, Germany
David Wilkins, Language and Linguistics Consulting, Australia

Table of Contents

Workshop Program

Thursday, June 7th, 2012

Joint Demo and Poster Session, together with the Workshop on Predicting and Improving Text Readability for Target Reader Populations (PITR 2012)

15:30–17:30 Coffee, system demonstrations, and posters

A free and open-source tool that reads movie subtitles aloud
Peter Ljunglöf, Sandra Derbring and Maria Olsson

WinkTalk: a demonstration of a multimodal speech synthesis platform linking facial expressions to expressive synthetic voices
Eva Szekely, Zeeshan Ahmed, Joao P. Cabral and Julie Carson-Berndsen

(plus posters of the regular papers from SLPAT and PITR)

17:30–18:30 SIG-SLPAT business meeting

Friday, June 8th, 2012

08:30–09:00 Registration

09:00–09:10 Opening remarks

Regular Paper Session

09:10–09:35 *Discourse-Based Modeling for AAC*
Margaret Mitchell and Richard Sproat

09:35–10:00 *Applying Prediction Techniques to Phoneme-based AAC Systems*
Ha Trinh, Annalu Waller, Keith Vertanen, Per Ola Kristensson and Vicki L. Hanson

10:00–10:25 *Non-Syntactic Word Prediction for AAC*
Karl Wiegand and Rupal Patel

10:30–11:00 Coffee break

Friday, June 8th, 2012 (continued)

User Panel

11:00–11:50 Invited user panel

Regular Paper Session

11:50–12:15 *Assisting Social Conversation between Persons with Alzheimer's Disease and their Conversational Partners*
Nancy Green, Curry Guinn and Ronnie Smith

12:15–12:40 *Communication strategies for a computerized caregiver for individuals with Alzheimer's disease*
Frank Rudzicz, Rozanne Wilson, Alex Mihailidis, Elizabeth Rochon and Carol Leonard

12:40–14:00 Lunch break

Regular Paper Session

14:00–14:25 *Generating Situated Assisting Utterances to Facilitate Tactile-Map Understanding: A Prototype System*
Kris Lohmann, Ole Eichhorn and Timo Baumann

14:25–14:50 *Learning a Vector-Based Model of American Sign Language Inflecting Verbs from Motion-Capture Data*
Pengfei Lu and Matt Huenerfauth

14:50–15:15 *A Hybrid System for Spanish Text Simplification*
Stefan Bott, Horacio Saggion and David Figueroa

Closing

15:15–15:30 Closing remarks

15:30– Coffe break, mingling, brainstorming, and mutual admiration

A free and open-source tool that reads movie subtitles aloud

Peter Ljunglöf
Computer Science and Engineering
University of Gothenburg
Gothenburg, Sweden
peter.ljunglof@gu.se

Sandra Derbring and **Maria Olsson**
DART: Centre for AAC and AT
Gothenburg, Sweden
sandra.derbring@vgregion.se
maria.in.olsson@vgregion.se

Abstract

We present a simple tool that enables the computer to read subtitles of movies and TV shows aloud. The tool extracts information from subtitle files, which can be freely downloaded from the Internet, and reads the text aloud through a speech synthesizer. There are three versions of the tool, one for Windows and Linux, another for Mac OS X, and the third is a browser-based HTML5 prototype. The tools are freely available and open-source.

The target audience is people who have trouble reading subtitles while watching a movie, including elderly, people with visual impairments, people with reading difficulties and people who wants to learn a second language. The application is currently being evaluated together with user from these groups.

1 Background

1.1 Why read subtitles aloud?

Spoken subtitles could be a solution if, due to sight disorder or poor reading skills, a person is unable to read subtitles and the language spoken in the movie is unknown, or not known well enough.

Swedish Association of the Visually Impaired[1] has around 12,000 members but there are most likely many more people with poor eyesight. The number of people with reading disabilities is unknown, but according to the Swedish dyslexia association "Dyslexiföreningen"[2] between 5 and 8 percent of the population have significant difficulties to read and write. A survey by OECD (Organisation for Economic Co-operation and Development) in 1996 showed that "8 per cent of the adult population [in Sweden] encounters a severe literacy deficit in everyday life and at work" (OECD, 2000, p. xiii). For other countries, the problems were even bigger: "In 14 out of 20 countries, at least 15 per cent of all adults have literacy skills at only the most rudimentary level" (OECD, 2000, p. xiii).

To hear the subtitles along with the original audio track of the movie may not suit everyone, but making these movies and TV shows accessible could bring a huge value for people who would use it.

1.2 Related work

The idea of automatic reading of movie and TV subtitles is not new. It is implemented in regular public service TV broadcasts in at least Sweden and the Netherlands, and probably also in more countries. In 2002, the Dutch national broadcasting company NOS started regular broadcasts of automatic subtitles reading (Verboom et al., 2002), and Sweden's public service TV company SVT followed in 2005 (A-focus, 2010, p. 20). In both these cases, the speech signal is transmitted through a second channel, which means that the user needs two digital boxes. Naturally, this solution only works for the programs that the company itself is broadcasting.

Other projects have been trying to use OCR (optical character recognition) to interpret the subtitles on the TV or computer screen. In 2002, a project by the Swedish Association of the Visually Impaired developed a prototype that used OCR to Interpret subtitles, which then were spoken aloud using TTS (Eliasson, 2005, pp. 63–64). The project estimated that a mass-produced product would cost around 2500€, which they concluded would be too much

[1] Synskadades riksförbund, http://www.srfriks.org/

[2] Dyslexiföreningen, http://dyslexiforeningen.se/

for ordinary users. In 2007, a similar Danish project described a tool that reads the composite video signal, performs OCR on the subtitles and then speaks them using TTS (Nielson and Bothe, 2007). They also developed a specialised OCR algorithm for subtitle detection (Jønsson and Bothe, 2007). However, both systems have remained prototypes and have not been released as publicly available tools.

A similar Czech project has investigated how to minimise speech overlap and how to get better synchronisation by using techniques such as time compression and text simplification (Hanzlíček et al., 2008; Matoušek et al., 2010). Their evaluation is purely technical, where they count the number of overlapped subtitles and the number of subtitles that require different compression factors, but they have not evaluated their prototype system on actual users.

Finally, there is an ongoing Swedish project by the Swedish dyslexia association "Dyslexiförbundet FMLS" where they aim to make cinemas more accessible by transmitting spoken subtitles via Wi-Fi which the users can listen to via their own mobile phone.

1.3 Issues with existing solutions

Currently there are two kinds of spoken subtitles systems, and both of them have different problems:

- TV broadcasting systems that transmit the spoken subtitles in a separate audio stream. It is an important addition to the TV infrastructure, but it is by nature closed to one media channel and cannot be used for users who want to watch movies or TV shows on their computer or from the Internet.

- Systems that use OCR to interpret movie subtitles have a great potential, but they are currently no publicly available systems. There are still some technological problems left to be solved until OCR based systems can be released to the public.

None of the existing systems are freely available, let alone open-source products. Furthermore, we have not found any studies that evaluate these systems on real users, to find out how useful they are in practice.

The systems we describe in this paper are all freely available and open-source. They are focused on personal computer use, not TV or cinemas, and are meant to be usable and easily installable to those with basic computer skills.

2 Implementation

The idea behind all our implementations is very simple. The program reads the subtitles into an internal database. When the movie starts playing, the program communicates with the movie to get the current time position, and calls a speech synthesiser when it is time to show the next subtitle. The program does not include a speech synthesiser, but assumes that it is already installed on the computer. Alternatively, the program can call an online web service-based TTS.

We have developed three systems which work in different ways and on different operating systems. Some of them are still in prototype/demo state, whereas others are almost finished products. All systems are free and open-source and can be downloaded from the project website:

http://code.google.com/p/subtts

2.1 Windows/Linux media player

The Windows/Linux client has been developed by the company STTS.[3] It is implemented in Python and the wxWidgets GUI toolkit.[4] The video playback interface uses a Python backend that comes with the VLC Media Player.[5] This means that the client can play all media formats that the VLC player can handle, including DVD movies.

2.2 Mac OS X menulet

The Mac OS X client uses the AppleScript Event model to communicate with the active media player. The program is developed in Objective-C and resides in the menu bar as a global "menulet"[6].

When the user starts watching a movie, the menulet repeatedly queries the media player for the current time, and calls the speech synthesiser whenever a new subtitle is about to be shown. The menulet currently supports the following media players: VLC, QuickTime Player (versions 7 and X), and Apple DVD Player.

[3] Södermalms Talteknologiservice, http://stts.se/
[4] wxWidgets, http://wxwidgets.org/
[5] VLC, http://videolan.org/
[6] http://en.wikipedia.org/wiki/Menulet

2.3 Browser-based HTML5 media player

We have also developed a prototype browser-based media player written in Javascript, that uses HTML5 video and audio elements to support spoken subtitles. This has the potential to be very useful, but is currently limited since current browsers do not support HTML5 video and audio in full.

We estimate that, in a few years time, the main browsers will support all HTML5 features,as well as offline TTS. Then this kind of HTML5 media player could have a big impact on movie and TV accessibility.

2.4 Subtitle files

The system does not extract the subtitles from the movie file or the DVD. Instead the user has to provide it with a text file with the movie subtitles. Subtitles are available from several sites on the Internet,[7] both in the original language and in translations into different other languages.

The subtitle format that we support is SRT, which is the de-facto standard for movie subtitiles and a very simple text format. Each subtitle is in a separate paragraph on the following form:

```
26
00:03:05,083 --> 00:03:09,417
You, I mean we,
we could easily die out here.
```

The above example means that the 26th subtitle consists of two lines of text, and should be displayed 3 minutes 5.083 seconds into the movie and disappear 4.334 seconds later.

Both the Windows and the Mac OS X clients can show DVD movies, but they cannot use the subtitles that are provided with the movie. DVD subtitles are pre-rendered into separate video tracks. To access them we would have to use OCR which was not in the scope of this project.

One serious drawback with existing subtitles is that they do not store meta-information about the speaker. Useful meta-information would be gender, age and dialect of the speaker, or even a unique identifier for each person in the movie. With this information the system could use different TTS voices for different characters.

[7]E.g., http://opensubtitles.org/ and http://undertexter.se/.

2.5 Speech synthesis

We are only using existing speech synthesisers, which means that the user either has to have a TTS voice installed on his/her computer, or constant access to the Internet since the system can call existing online TTS engines. The only problem with online TTS systems is that almost all of them are for demonstration purposes only and therefore cannot be used in day-to-day work. We have been using an online Swedish open-source voice being developed by the company STTS[8] using the OpenMary TTS platform (Schröder and Trouvain, 2003).

Here is the current status of speech synthesis for our different systems:

- The Windows client can use any SAPI voice installed on the system. It can also use an online voice, as an alternative.
- The Mac OS X client can use any voice installed on the system. The latest version of OS X (10.7) includes high-quality voices for 22 different languages, so there is no need for online voices on this platform.
- The HTML5 browser client cannot use system-installed voices, since that functionality is not included in HTML5. There is a current W3C draft proposal for how to use TTS from within HTML (Bringert, 2010), but it is not decided upon and no browsers support this yet. Until TTS becomes a HTML standard we have to rely on online voices, which unfortunately is a scarce resource.

3 Discussion

3.1 Social and pedagogical advantages

People with visually impairments and/or reading difficulties often use text-to-speech to cope with school work, and to keep up with society. Spoken subtitles further increase the accessibility of foreign movies and TV shows for these people.

Hopefully, spoken subtitles can help improve the reading skills for people with reading difficulties. The theory is that listening to the spoken subtitles at the same time as reading the text may benefit the reading process, but this has yet to be tested.

[8]Södermalms Talteknologiservice, http://stts.se/

3.2 Evaluation

We are currently, during spring 2012, evaluating the applications together with different users in the target groups. Initially we will only be evaluating user satisfaction and whether this approach could be an accepted solution to the need of text interpretation during movie playback.

If this initial evaluation is positive, we are very interested in continuing by evaluating specific factors that might or might not improve user satisfaction. Such factors could be: using different TTS voices, using different speech rates, reducing speech overlap, having the speech coming from another direction, lowering the movie volume while speaking, using advanced audio techniques for filtering away movie speech, etc.

Another interesting evaluation would be to encode speaker meta-information into movie subtitles, and test how different TTS voices for different characters can improve the user's satisfaction and comprehension.

3.3 Future work

To further ease the user friendliness and the availability, it would be desirable to have the functionality built into an existing media player, such as the open-source and cross-platform VLC Media Player.[9] If more users request this functionality, the developers will have to catch on and include it into new releases.

According to (Hanzlíček et al., 2008), 44 percent of the Czech subtitles had overlaps when spoken with TTS. Even though we have no figures for Swedish, some overlap is to be expected also here, which is an issue that should be addressed. One possible simple solution is to modify the speech rate.

An important factor for the experience of the speech synthesizer together with a video playback would be the settings of the audio channels. Hypothetically, a listener would want to keep both the original background cues, like music, and the original voices. However, these sounds must not interfere with the speech synthesizer that is the source of information for the listener. Balancing these two criteria to get the optimized result is of great interest.

If the program would be used for language learning, or to help slow readers to comprehend, the feature of highlighting the word that is spoken could be a very useful additional feature.

Acknowledgements

The SubTTS project is funded by the Swedish Post and Telecom Authority (PTS). We are grateful to four anonymous referees for their comments.

References

A-focus. 2010. *Utredning avseende TV-tillgänglighet för personer med funktionsnedsättning*. Myndigheten för radio och TV, Stockholm, Sweden.

Björn Bringert. 2010. HTML text to speech (TTS) API specification. W3c editor's draft, W3C.

Folke Eliasson. 2005. *IT i praktiken – slutrapport*. Hjälpmedelsinstitutet, Sweden.

Zdeněk Hanzlíček, Jindřich Matoušek, and Daniel Tihelka. 2008. Towards automatic audio track generation for Czech TV broadcasting: Initial experiments with subtitles-to-speech synthesis. In *ICSP '08, 9th International Conference on Signal Processing*, Beijing, China.

Morten Jønsson and Hans Heinrich Bothe. 2007. OCR-algorithm for detection of subtitles in television and cinema. In *CVHI'07, 5th Conference and Workshop on Assistive Technology for People with Vision and Hearing Impairments*, Granada, Spain.

Jindřich Matoušek, Zdeněk Hanzlíček, Daniel Tihelka, and Martin Méner. 2010. Automatic dubbing of TV programmes for the hearing impaired. In *10th IEEE International Conference on Signal Processing*, Beijing, China.

Simon Nielson and Hans Heinrich Bothe. 2007. SubPal: A device for reading aloud subtitles from television and cinema. In *CVHI'07, 5th Conference and Workshop on Assistive Technology for People with Vision and Hearing Impairments*, Granada, Spain.

OECD. 2000. *Literacy in the Information Age: Final Report of the International Adult Literacy Survey*. OECD Publications, Paris.

Marc Schröder and Jürgen Trouvain. 2003. The German text-to-speech synthesis system MARY: A tool for research, development and teaching. *International Journal of Speech Technology*, 6:365–377.

Maarten Verboom, David Crombie, Evelien Dijk, and Mildred Theunisz. 2002. Spoken subtitles: Making subtitled TV programmes accessible. In *ICCHP'02, 8th International Conference on Computers Helping People with Special Needs*, Linz, Austria.

[9] VLC Media Player, http://www.videolan.org/vlc/

WinkTalk: a demonstration of a multimodal speech synthesis platform linking facial expressions to expressive synthetic voices

Éva Székely, Zeeshan Ahmed, João P. Cabral, Julie Carson-Berndsen
CNGL, School of Computer Science and Informatics, University College Dublin
Belfield, D4, Dublin, Ireland
{eva.szekely|zeeshan.ahmed}@ucdconnect.ie,{joao.cabral|julie.berndsen}@ucd.ie

Abstract

This paper describes a demonstration of the WinkTalk system, which is a speech synthesis platform using expressive synthetic voices. With the help of a webcamera and facial expression analysis, the system allows the user to control the expressive features of the synthetic speech for a particular utterance with their facial expressions. Based on a personalised mapping between three expressive synthetic voices and the users facial expressions, the system selects a voice that matches their face at the moment of sending a message. The WinkTalk system is an early research prototype that aims to demonstrate that facial expressions can be used as a more intuitive control over expressive speech synthesis than manual selection of voice types, thereby contributing to an improved communication experience for users of speech generating devices.

1 Introduction

During a human verbal communication process, expressive features of face and speech are congruent, operating in a synchronised manner (Campbell, 2008), (Graf et al., 2002). Facial expressions and expressive speech styles often help to convey the emotional intent of the speaker that is only partially contained in the words. The application described in this paper aims to make use of this synchrony and applies facial expressions as a real time volitional control over the expressive features of synthetic utterance productions of augmented speakers. The WinkTalk system is currently a research prototype in progress, operating on a personal computer equipped with a webcamera. The goal of the system is to respond to the need of integrated multimodality in speech generating devices of users of augmentative and alternative communication[1] (AAC) applications (Higginbotham, 2010). Being able to correctly link facial expression to synthetic speech output is a step forward to a more intuitive way of controlling the expressiveness of synthetic speech. The approach can be considered novel, as the authors are not aware of another system using facial expressions to control expressive TTS.

2 WinkTalk system architecture

The WinkTalk system is a web based application developed using AJAX and PHP technologies. The web application provides a flexible interface and allows for easy integration of new components such as synthetic voices or gesture recognisers running on a web server. The internal architecture of the system is shown in figure 1. The system operates based on a configurable workflow defining the three modes of the system: a personalisation mode, an automatic voice selection mode based on facial expression, which is the core functionality of the system, and a control mode of manual voice selection, that was included for evaluation purposes. In the manual voice selection application the user is presented with the three options and selects the voice style that

[1] Augmentative and alternative communication (AAC) refers to an area of research, clinical, and educational practice. AAC involves attempts to study and when necessary compensate for temporary or permanent impairments, activity limitations, and participation restrictions of individuals with severe disorders of speech-language production and/or comprehension, including spoken and written modes of communication.(ASHA, 2005)

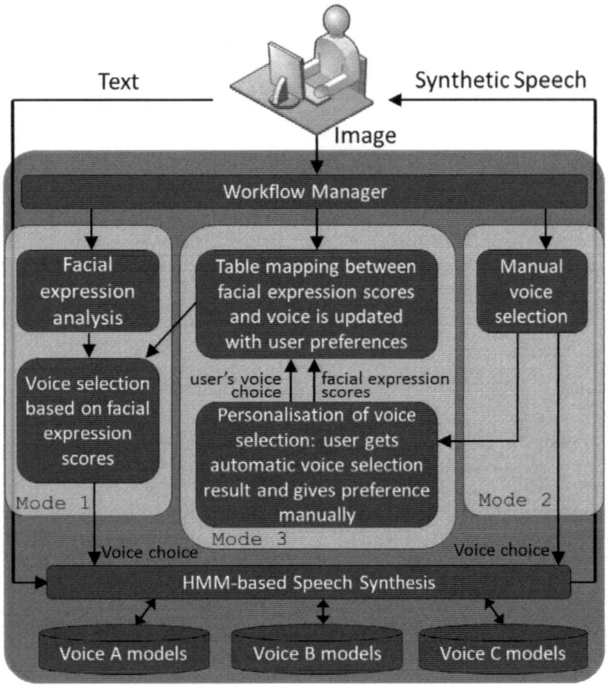

Figure 1: Architecture and working modes of the WinkTalk system

matches the emotional or expressive intent of the message. It has previously been shown that after a short familiarisation with the voices, it is possible for the user to make a fairly good prediction of how a particular utterance will sound when synthesised with one of the voices (Székely et al., 2012). This makes it possible to use the system in a conversation situation, in which the user does not have the opportunity to listen to the three possible speech samples but needs to make a choice ahead of the time of the synthesis. The automatic voice choice mode and the personalisation mode will be described in sections 3 and 4, respectively.

3 Facial expression based voice selection

3.1 Expressive synthetic voices

The synthesiser component of the application uses three expressive HMM-based synthetic voices of a middle aged American male. The voices have been built using the HTS speech engine 2.1., from an audiobook corpus made available for Blizzard Challenge 2012 by Toshiba Research Europe Ltd, Cambridge Research Laboratory. Each synthetic voice was trained from different subcorpora of the audiobook obtained using an unsupervised clustering technique based on glottal source parameters (Székely et al., 2011). Perceptual experiments have shown (Hennig et al., 2012) that the three voices can be characterised on an expressiveness gradient: from calm (A voice), through intense (B voice) to very intense (C voice). This expressiveness gradient can be described with characteristics such as with rising pitch, greater prosodic variation, increased power and voice quality changing from lax to tense.

3.2 Facial expression analysis

For facial expression recognition, the system uses the Sophisticated Highspeed Object Recognition Engine (SHORE) library by Fraunhofer. To detect faces and expressions, SHORE analyses local structure features in images and outputs scores for four distinct facial expressions: *happy, sad, angry* and *surprised*, with an indication of the intensity of the expression (Kueblbeck and Ernst, 2006). The intensity ranges from 0-100, a higher value meaning a more intense expression in that category.

3.3 Mapping between facial expressions and voices

The system uses the facial expression categories and intensity scores outputted by SHORE to select from the three synthetic voices. The initial mapping between facial expression categories and ranges of intensity values and voices are shown in Table 1. For example, an image analysed as containing the facial expression *suprised* with an intensity of 25, the system will synthesise the corresponding utterance with the C voice. The system always uses the facial expression category with the highest value for a particular image. These initial values have been

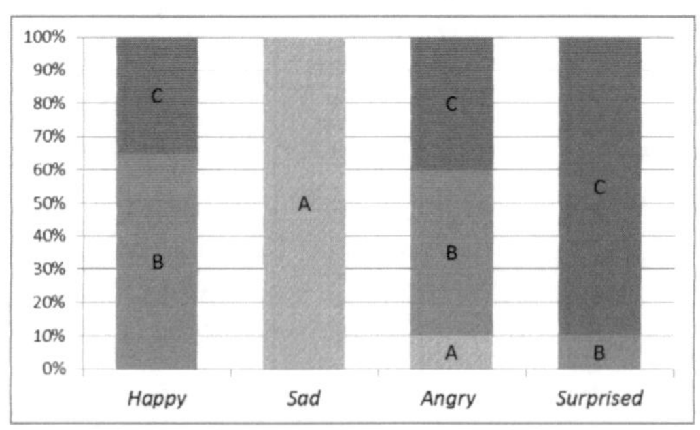

Figure 2: Initial thresholds for mapping different intensity values of the facial expressions to the synthetic voices

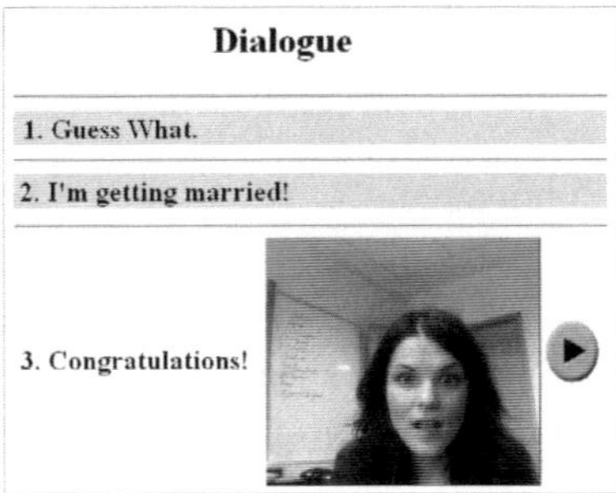

Figure 3: Interface of the dialogue simulation with WinkTalk.

chosen based on considerations about arousal levels of the underlying basic emotion of the facial expression categories, for example with surprise being a high arousal emotion, the intensity scores of it result sooner in a higher intensity voice choice. The values have also been supported by the results a perceptual test carried out by 25 participants on a dataset that was balanced to contain equal amount of stimuli from all facial expression categories. Participants were asked to select from three synthesised utterances the one best matching the facial expression of a person on a picture. The perceptual test has shown that 90% of all majority votings (above 66% agreement among participants) fell within the initial threshold values. When a message is being sent to the synthesiser, the system makes a snapshot of the user's face. Based on the image scores and threshold table, the system decides which voice best suits the current facial expression and returns the results accordingly. The system also provides an option to take streaming video input from the camera rather than a single image, and calculate the feature values over an interval of the video around the time of sending a message. To take into consideration the cases where individual preferences of voice choice differ greatly, as well as to account for individual differences in facial characteristics, a personalisation component has been integrated in the system, which will be introduced in section 4.

4 Personalisation component

In order to optimise the performance of the WinkTalk system, a personalisation session needs to be completed by each user. The objective of the personalisation is to adjust the voice selection threshold according to users' facial characteristics and individual preferences. In the personalisation phase,

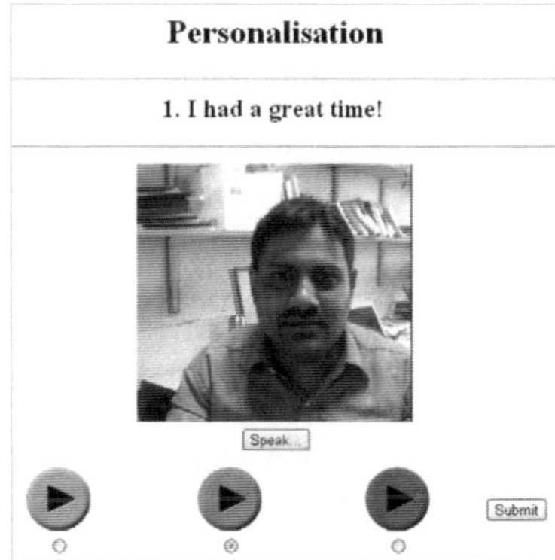

Figure 4: Interface of the personalisation component of WinkTalk.

the user is presented with a sentence and makes an appropriate facial expression to accompany the utterance. The facial expression is captured and analysed by the system and the user is presented with the three options of synthetic speech samples, along with an indication of which sample the system chose to match their facial expression. If the user does not agree with the selection provided by the system, a preference can be indicated by choosing from the other two options. The system then adjusts the threshold by moving it by a standard factor towards the outlying training example. The new threshold is applied in next trial. The thresholds for each facial expression-voice pair are normalised so that there is no overlap between the different voices for the same feature.

5 Conclusions and future work

The WinkTalk system has been evaluated within an interactive evaluation session involving 10 subjects, each of them acting out pre-scripted dialogues with a conversation partner. The evaluation has shown that while there is a general preference to manual selection of expressive voices, 90% of the participants described facial expression control as a valuable addition to the simulated augmented communication process. A strong learning effect in the ease of using the system has also been observed. Future work is planned to research further input strategies of gestures as well as to integrate a female expressive synthetic voice. An essential next step is to extend the personalisation component to include the possibility of fully personalised training of the facial expression analysis to fit individual needs of users who are restricted with respect to their gestural expressiveness.

6 Demonstration

6.1 Overview

The demonstration will give participants an opportunity to use the WinkTalk system by conducting the personalisation phase and using the system with pre-scripted dialogues. It is intended for those interested in using multimodal tools and expressive speech to improve the communication experience of individuals with complex communication needs. The demonstration will give participants a chance to experience the facial expression control over the voice choice of the system as well as get an impression of how the range of expressive voices can be used in an acted dialogue situation. A 3 minute video of the system in use will also be available for viewing.

6.2 Familiarisation/Personalisation phase

First, a short introduction will be given to the system and its aims, then the participants will be introduced to the synthetic voices by listening to a few samples receiving a brief description of their characteristics. Subsequently, the participants will be asked to conduct a personalisation session including 20 iterations, that will help optimise the system to adapt to the participants' preferences, as described in section 4. It will also familiarise the users with the characteristics of the voices and the mapping of facial expressions and voices.

6.3 Dialogue simulation with synthetic voices

After the users are familiarised with the system, they can choose from a set of 8 dialogues representing a range of social interactions and emotional sentiment and intensity. Participants will act out some of the dialogues with a conversation partner, using facial expressions to control the selection of the synthetic voices instead of speaking with their own voice. They will also have the option to compare the facial expression control of the WinkTalk system with a simple manual selection of synthetic voices for each utterance. At the end of the dialogue session there will be a chance to fill out a feedback form to help the further development of the system.

Acknowledgments

This research is supported by the Science Foundation Ireland (Grant 07/CE/I1142) as part of the Centre for Next Generation Localisation (www.cngl.ie) at University College Dublin (UCD). The opinions, findings, and conclusions or recommendations expressed in this material are those of the authors and do not necessarily reflect the views of Science Foundation Ireland. The authors would also like to thank Shannon Hennig (IIT), Nick Campbell and the Speech Communication Lab (TCD), for their invaluable help with the interactive evaluation.

References

American Speech-Language-Hearing Association. 2005 *Roles and Responsibilities of Speech-Language Pathologists With Respect to Augmentative and Alternative Communication: Position Statement.* Available from www.asha.org/policy.

Campbell, N. 2008. *Multimodal processing of discourse information; the effect of synchrony* Proc. of International Symposium on Universal Communication, Osaka.

Graf, H.P., Cosatto, E., Strom, V., and Huang, F.J. 2002. *Visual prosody: Facial movements accompanying speech.* Proc. of the 5th International Conference on Automatic Face and Gesture Recognition.

Hennig, S., Székely, É., Carson-Berndsen, J. and Chellali, R. 2012. *Listener evaluation of an expressiveness scale in speech synthesis for conversational phrases: implications for AAC.* to appear in: Proc. of ISAAC, Pittsburgh.

Higginbotham, D. J. 2010. *Humanizing Vox Artificialis: The Role of Speech Synthesis in Augmentative and Alternative Communication* Computer Synthesized Speech Technologies: Tools for Aiding Impairment, J. Mullennix and S. Stern, Eds. IGI Global, pp. 50-70.

HTS-2.1 toolkit, HMM-based speech synthesis system version 2.1. http://hts.sp.nitech.ac.jp.

Kueblbeck., C. and Ernst, A. 2006. *Face detection and tracking in video sequences using the modified census transformation.* Journal on Image and Vision Computing, vol. 24, issue 6, pp. 564-572.

SHORE face detection engine, Fraunhofer Institute http://www.iis.fraunhofer.de/en/bf/bsy/fue/isyst

Székely, É., Cabral, J., Abou-Zleikha, M., Cahill, P. and Carson-Berndsen, J. 2012. *Evaluating expressive speech synthesis from audiobook corpora for conversational phrases.* Proc. of LREC, Istanbul.

Székely, É., Cabral, J. P., Cahill, P. and Carson-Berndsen, J. 2011. *Clustering expressive speech styles in audiobooks using glottal source parameters.* Proc. of Interspeech, Florence.

Discourse-Based Modeling for AAC

Margaret Mitchell **Richard Sproat**
Center for Spoken Language Understanding
Oregon Health & Science University
m.mitchell@abdn.ac.uk, rws@xoba.com

Abstract

This paper presents a method for an AAC system to predict a whole response given features of the previous utterance from the interlocutor. It uses a large corpus of scripted dialogs, computes a variety of lexical, syntactic and whole phrase features for the previous utterance, and predicts features that the response should have, using an entropy-based measure. We evaluate the system on a held-out portion of the corpus. We find that for about 3.5% of cases in the held-out corpus, we are able to predict a response, and among those, over half are either exact or at least reasonable substitutes for the actual response. We also present some results on keystroke savings. Finally we compare our approach to a state-of-the-art *chatbot*, and show (not surprisingly) that a system like ours, tuned for a particular style of conversation, outperforms one that is not.

Predicting possible responses automatically by mining a corpus of dialogues is a novel contribution to the literature on whole utterance-based methods in AAC. Also useful, we believe, is our estimate that about 3.5-4.0% of utterances in dialogs are in principle predictable given previous context.

1 Introduction

One of the overarching goals of Augmentative and Alternative Communication technology is to help impaired users communicate more quickly and more naturally. Over the past thirty years, solutions that attempt to reduce the amount of effort needed to input a sentence have include semantic compaction (Baker, 1990), and lexicon- or language-model-based word prediction (Darragh et al., 1990; Higginbotham, 1992; Li and Hirst, 2005; Trost et al., 2005; Trnka et al., 2006; Trnka et al., 2007; Wandmacher and Antoine, 2007), among others. In recent years, there has been an increased interest in whole utterance-based and discourse-based approaches (see Section 2). Such approaches have been argued to be beneficial in that they can speed up the conversation, thus making it appear more felicitous (McCoy et al., 2007). Most commercial tablets sold as AAC devices contain an inventory of canned phrases, comprising such items as common greetings, polite phrases, salutations and so forth. Users can also enter their own phrases, or indeed entire sequences of phrases (e.g., for a prepared talk).

The work presented here attempts to take whole phrase prediction one step further by automatically predicting appropriate responses to utterances by mining conversational text. In an actual deployment, one would present a limited number of predicted phrases in a prominent location on the user's device, along with additional input options. The user could then select from these phrases, or revert to other input methods. In actual use, one would also want such a system to incorporate speech recognition (ASR), but for the present we restrict ourselves to typed text — which is perfectly appropriate for some modes of interaction such as on-line social media domains. Using a corpus of 72 million words from American soap operas, we isolate features useful in predicting an appropriate set of responses for the previous utterance of an interlocutor. The main results of this work are a method that can automatically produce appropriate responses to utterances in some cases, and an estimate of what percentage of dialog may be amenable to such techniques.

2 Previous Work

Alm et al. (1992) discuss how AAC technology can increase social interaction by having the utterance, rather than the letter or word, be the basic unit of communication. Findings from conversational analysis suggest a number of utterances common to conversation, including short conversational openers and closers (*hello*, *goodbye*), backchannel responses (*yeah?*), and quickfire phrases (*That's too bad.*). Indeed "small talk" is central to smooth-flowing conversation (King et al., 1995). Many modern AAC systems therefore provide canned small-talk phrases (Alm et al., 1993; Todman et al., 2008).

More complex conversational utterances are challenging to predict, and recent systems have used a variety of approaches to generate longer phrases from minimal user input. One approach relies on telegraphic input, where full sentences are constructed from a set of uninflected words, as in the Compansion system (McCoy et al., 1998). This system employs a semantic parser to capture the meaning of the input words and generates using the Functional Unification Formalism (FUF) system (Elhadad, 1991). One of the limitations of this approach is that information associated with each word is primarily hand-coded on the basis of intuition; as a result, the system cannot handle the problem of unrestricted vocabulary. Similar issues arise in semantic authoring systems (Netzer and Elhadad, 2006), where at each step of the sentence creation process, the system offers possible symbols for a small set of concepts, and the user can select which is intended.

Recent work has also tried to handle the complexity of conversation by providing full sentences with slots that can be filled in by the user. Dempster et al. (2010) define an ontology where pieces of hand-coded knowledge are stored and realized within several syntactic templates. Users can generate utterances by entering utterance types and topics, and these are filled into the templates. The Frametalker system (Higginbotham et al., 1999) uses contextual frames — basic sentences for different contexts — with a set vocabulary for each. The intuition behind this system is that there are typical linguistic structures for different situations and the kinds of words that the user will need to fill in will be semantically related to the context. Wisenburn and Higginbotham (2008) extend this technology using ASR on the speech of the interlocutor. The system extracts noun phrases from the speech and presents those noun phrases on the AAC device, with frame sentences that the user can then select. Thus, if the interlocutor says *Paris*, the AAC user will be able to select from phrases like *Tell me more about Paris* or *I want to talk about Paris*.

Other approaches provide a way for users to quickly find canned utterances. WordKeys (Langer and Hickey, 1998) allows users to access stored phrases by entering key words. This system approaches generation as a text retrieval task, using a lexicon derived from WordNet to expand user input to find possible utterances. Dye et al. (1998) introduce a system that utilizes scripts for specific situations. Although pre-stored scripts work reasonably well for specific contexts, the authors find (not unexpectedly) that a larger number of scripts are needed for the system to be generally effective.

3 The Soap Opera Corpus

In this work we attempt a different approach, developing a system that can learn appropriate responses to utterances given a corpus of conversations.

Part of the difficulty in automatically generating conversational utterances is that very large corpora of naturally occurring dialogs are non-existent. The closest such corpus is Switchboard (Godfrey and Holliman, 1997), which contains 2,400 two-sided conversations with about 1.4 million words. The interlocutors in Switchboard are not acquainted with each other and they are instructed to discuss a particular topic. While the dialogs are "natural" to a point, because they involve people who have never previously met, they are not particularly reflective of the kinds of conversations between intimates that we are interested in helping impaired users with.

We thus look instead to a corpus of scripted dialogs taken from American soap operas. The website `tvmegasite.net` contains soap opera scripts that have been transcribed by aficionados of the various series. The scripts include utterances marked with information on which character is speaking, and a few dramatic cues. We downloaded 72 million words of text, with 5.5 million utterances. Soap opera series downloaded were: *All my Children*, *As the World Turns*, *The Bold and the Beautiful*, *Days of our Lives*, *General Hospital*, *Guiding Light*, *One Life to Live* and *The Young and the Restless*. The text was cleaned to remove HTML markup and other extraneous material, and the result was a set of 550,000 dialogs, with alternating utterances by (usually) two speakers. These dialogs were split 0.8/0.1/0.1 into training, development testing and testing portions, respectively. All results reported in this paper are on the *development test set*.

While soap operas may not be very representative of most people's lives, the corpus nonetheless has three advantages. First of all, the corpus is large. Second, the language tends to be fairly colloquial. Third, many of the dialogs take place between characters who are supposed to know each other well, often intimately; thus the topics might be more reflective of casual conversation between friends and intimates than the dialogs one finds in Switchboard.

4 Data Analysis, Feature Extraction and Utterance Prediction

Each dialog was processed using the Stanford Core NLP tools. The Stanford tools perform part of speech tagging (Toutanova et al., 2003), constituent and dependency parsing (Klein and Manning, 2003), named entity recognition (Finkel et al., 2005), and coreference resolution (Lee et al., 2011). From the output of the Stanford tools, the following features were extracted for each utterance: *word bigrams* (pairs of adjacent words); *dependency-head relations*, along with the type of dependency relation (basically, governors — e.g., verbs — and their dependents — e.g., nouns); *named entities* (persons, organizations, etc.); and *the whole utterance*. Extracted named entities include noun phrases that were explicitly tagged as named entities, as well as any phrases that were marked as coreferential with named entities. Thus if the pronoun *she* occurred in an utterance, and was marked as coreferential with a previous or following named entity *Amelia*, then the feature *Amelia* as a named entity was added for this utterance. We also include the whole utterance as a feature, which turns out to be the most useful predictor for an appropriate response to an input utterance.

The dialogs were divided into turns, with each turn consisting of one or more utterances. For our experiments, we are interested in predicting the *first utterance* of a turn (which in many cases may be the whole turn) *given features of all the utterances of the previous turns* — the exception being that for the whole sentence feature, only the last sentence of the previous turn is used. The method of using features of a turn to predict features of the next turn is related to the work reported in Purandare and Litman (2008), though their goal was to analyze dialog coherence rather than to predict the next utterance.

We are particularly interested in feature values that are highly skewed in their predictions, meaning that if the turn has a given value, then the first sentence of the next utterance is much more likely to have some values than others. A useful measure of this is the difference between the entropy of the predicted feature values f_i of a feature g:

$$H(g) = -\sum_{i=0}^{n} \log(p(f_i)) \cdot p(f_i) \qquad (1)$$

and the maximum possible entropy of g given n predicted features, namely:

$$H_{max}(g) = -\log(\frac{1}{n}) \qquad (2)$$

The larger the difference $H_{max}(g) - H(g)$, the more skewed the distribution.

For the purposes of this experiment and to keep the computation reasonably tractable, we computed the entropic values described above for like features: thus we used bigram features to predict bigram features, dependency features to predict dependency features, and so forth. We also filtered the output of the process so that each feature of the prior context had a minimum of 10 occurrences, and the entropy of the feature was no greater than 0.9 of the maximum entropy as defined above. For each feature value, the 2 most strongly associated values for the predicted utterance were stored.

To take a simple example (Figure 1) the bigram *'m fine* has a strong association with the bigrams *you 're* and *, I*, these co-occurring 486 and 464 times in the training corpus, respectively. For this feature, the

```
'm fine 8.196261 9.406976      you 're 486
'm fine 8.196261 9.406976      , i     464

you're kidding . __SENT 4.348040 4.852030
no. . __SENT 32
you're kidding . __SENT 4.348040 4.852030
i wish . __SENT 7
```

Figure 1: Examples of bigram and full-sentence features.

entropy is 8.20 and the maximum entropy is 9.41. Or consider a full-sentence feature *You're kidding*. This is strongly associated with the predicted sentence features *no..* and *I wish..*

Utterances in the training data were stored and associated with predicted features. In order to produce a rank-ordered list of possible responses to a test utterance, the features of the test utterance are extracted. For each of these features, the predicted features and their entropies are retrieved. Those training data utterances that match on one or more of these predicted features are retrieved in this step, and a score is assigned which is simply the sum of the predicted feature entropies. However, since we want to favor full-sentence matches, entropies for full-sentence matches are multiplied by a positive number (currently set to 100).

5 Experimental Results

5.1 Whole sentence prediction

The first question we were interested in is how often, based on the approach described here, one could predict a sentence that is close to what the speaker actually intended to say. For this purpose, we simply took as the gold standard the utterance that was written in the script for the speaker, and considered the prediction of the system described above, when it was able to make one. The prediction could be an exact match to what was actually said, something close enough to be a reasonable substitute, something appropriate given the context but not the one intended, or something that is wholly inappropriate.

In the ensuing discussion we will focus on whole sentence features, since these were the most useful for predicting reasonable whole sentences. We return to the use of other features in Section 5.2.

Some examples can be found in Figure 2. In each case, we give the final sentence of the previous turn, the actual utterance, and the two predicted utterances, along with the predicted utterances' scores and the counts with which they co-occurred in the training data with the previous utterance in question. For the first example *Really?*, the actual response was *Yeah*, and this was also the highest ranked response of the system. In the second example, the actual response was *I love you, too, baby doll*, whereas a response of the system was *I love you too*. While not exact, this is arguably close enough, and could be selected by an impaired user who did not wish to type the whole message. In the third example, the predictions *Yeah.* and *Ok.* do not substitute at all for the actual response.

```
PREV   really ?
ACTUAL yeah .
PRED   232.3099  yeah . __SENT 4
PRED   230.9528  mm-hmm . __SENT 3

PREV   love you .
ACTUAL i love you , too , baby doll .
PRED   83.4519 i love you , too . __SENT 3
PRED   74.1185 love you . __SENT 3

PREV   ok ?
ACTUAL i'm sorry , laurie , about j.r. ,
       about everything .
PRED   86.2623  yeah . __SENT 2
PRED   86.2623  ok . __SENT 2
```

Figure 2: Whole sentence prediction examples.

Of the 276,802 utterance-response pairs in the development test data, the system was able to make predictions for 9,794 cases, or 3.5%. Evaluating 9,794 responses is labor intensive, so two evaluations based on random samples were performed.

In the first, the authors evaluated a random sample of 455 utterance pairs, assigning the following scores to each response: **4** exact match; **3** equivalent meaning; **2** good answer but not the right one; **1** inappropriate. The results are given in Table 1, for the *best score* of the pair of responses generated. In other words, if the first response has a score of 2 and the second a score of 3, then the pair of responses will receive a score of 3: in that pair, there was one generated response that was close enough to use. From Table 1, we see that between 38% to 40.7% of the response pairs contained a response that was exact, or close enough to have the same meaning. 59.3% to 62% had at best a reasonable answer, but not the one intended. Finally, none contained only

Score	Judge 1		Judge 2	
Exact match	110	24.2%	109	24.0%
Equivalent meaning	63	13.8%	76	16.7%
Good answer (but wrong)	282	62.0%	270	59.3%
Inappropriate	0	0.0%	0	0.0%

Table 1: Judgments of a sample of 455 utterance pairs by the authors.

inappropriate answers: this is not surprising, given that all of the predicted responses were based on what was found in the training data, which one may assume involved largely felicitous interactions.

We also used Amazon's Mechanical Turk (AMT) to collect judgements from unbiased judges. Based on our previous evaluation, we expanded the *equivalent meaning* category into two more fine-grained categories, *essentially the same* and *similar meaning*, in order to capture phrases with slightly different connotations. This results in the 4-point scale in Table 2. Exact matches were found automatically before giving response pairs to Turkers, and account for a large portion of the data — 2,330 of the 9,794 response pairs, or 23.8%. For the remaining 76.2%, 138 participants were asked to judge how close the predicted response was to the actual response.

Each AMT participant was presented with six prompts (three entropy-based conversational turns and three chatbot-based conversational turns, discussed below). Each prompt listed the utterance, actual response, and predicted response. Two additional prompts with known answers were included to automatically flag participants who were not focusing on the task. Evaluation results are given in Table 3. Percentages are multiplied by the proportion of results they represent (.762). Of the evaluated cases, we find that 31.3% of the predicted responses were judged to be essentially the same or similar to the actual response. 30.4% were judged to be a reasonable answer, and the remaining 14.5% were judged to be inappropriate.

4 Essentially the same:	They're pretty close, and mean basically the same thing.
3 Similar meaning:	They're similar, but the predicted response has a slightly different connotation from the actual response.
2 Good answer, but not the right one:	They're different, but the predicted response is still a reasonable response to the comment.
1 Inappropriate:	Different, and the predicted response is a totally unreasonable response to the comment.

Table 2: Four-point scale for AMT evaluation. Exact matches were found automatically.

Essentially the same	89	16.4%
Similar meaning	81	14.9%
Good answer (but wrong)	165	30.4%
Inappropriate	79	14.5%

Table 3: Evaluation results from AMT on a random sample of 414 predicted utterances (excluding exact matches).

Evaluation by AMT judges was thus much more favorable towards the prediction-based system than the authors' evaluation. Where the authors found 13.8%-16.7% to be essentially the same or similar, unbiased judges found just under a third of the data to meet these criteria. Coupled with the automatically detected exact matches, 55.1% of the predicted responses were found to be a reasonable approximation of (or exactly) the intended response. A smaller portion of the data was thought to be a good answer (but wrong), or wholly inappropriate.

5.2 Prediction with features plus a prefix of the intended utterance

It is of course not necessary for the system to predict the whole response without any input from the user. As with word prediction, the user might type a *prefix* of the intended utterance, and the system could then produce a small set of corresponding responses, among which would often be the one desired.

In order to evaluate such a scenario, we considered the shortest prefix of the actual intended response that would be consistent with a maximum of five sentences predicted from the features of the previous turn. Thus, we gathered the entire set of sentences from the training data that matched one or more of the predicted features, then began (virtually) typing the actual response. There are two possible outcomes. If the actual response is not in the set, then at some point the typed prefix will be consistent with none of the sentences in the set. In this worst case, the user would simply have to type the whole sentence (possibly using whatever word-completion technology is already available on the device). But if the intended response is in the set, then at some point the set consistent with the prefix will be winnowed down to at most five members. The length of the prefix at that point, subtracted from the length of the intended sentence, is the keystroke savings.

Of the 276,802 utterances in the development test responses, 11,665 (4.2%) had a keystroke savings of greater than zero: thus, in 4.2% of cases, the intended utterance was to be found among the set of sentences consistent with the predicted features. The total keystroke savings was 102,323 characters out of a total of 8,725,508, or about 1%. While this is clearly small, note that it is over and above whatever keystroke savings one would gain by other methods, such as language modeling.

5.3 ALICE

A final experiment involved using a *chatbot* to generate responses. Previous approaches have used stored sentence templates that are generated based on keyword input from the user; a similar approach is used in a chatbot, where the input utterances are themselves triggers for the generated content. For this experiment, we used the publicly available ALICE (Wallace, 2012), which won the Loebner Prize (a Turing test) in 2000, 2001, and 2004. ALICE makes use of a large library of pattern-action pairs written in AIML (Artificial Intelligence Markup Language): if an input sentence matches a particular pattern, a response is generated by a rule that is associated with that pattern. ALICE follows conversational context by using a notion of TOPIC (what the conversation is currently about, based on keywords) and of THAT (the bot's previous utterance). Both are used along with the input utterance when selecting what next to say. In essence, ALICE is a much more sophisticated version of the 1960s Eliza program (Weizenbaum, 1966).

In order to use the chatbot for this task, we use an AIML interpreter (Stratton, 2010) on the most recent set of ALICE knowledge.[1] ALICE was given the utterances for each conversation in our development testing set, which allows the system to store some of the dialogue context under its THAT and TOPIC variables.

Essentially the same	45	10.7%
Similar meaning	96	22.9%
Good answer (but wrong)	135	32.1%
Inappropriate	138	32.9%

Table 4: Evaluation results from AMT on a random sample of 414 chatbot utterances (excluding exact matches).

Example responses are given in Figure 3. As with the previous experiments, some responses are close to the actual intended message (first example in Figure 3). In some other cases (second example), the response is reasonable, though not the one intended. But in many cases, the response is too "cute", as in the examples on the righthand side.

Evaluation with AMT is given in Table 4, using the same scoring criteria as in Table 3. Exact matches are again automatically removed, and account for 142 responses (1.5%). For the remaining data, participants were asked to judge how close the chatbot response was to the actual response. Percentages are multiplied by the proportion of results they represent (.9855).

The chatbot is judged to produce less acceptable utterances than the entropy-based approach, with 10.7% essentially the same as the actual response, and 22.9% with similar meaning. Coupled with the automatically detected exact matches, 35% of the chatbot responses were found to be a reasonable approximation of (or exactly) the intended response. Over half of the data (65%) was thought to be a good answer (but wrong), or wholly inappropriate.

6 Discussion and Future Work

Of the two different methods for automatically generating responses, the entropy-based approach in particular produces responses ranging from similar to exact in a majority of the cases for which it can make a prediction. These are promising findings for expanding a system that populates possible responses from an input utterance.

An obvious limitation of the work presented here is that it is based on scripted data. More to the point, to build an effective dialog-based system for an impaired user, the best possible data to use would be data involving the user him/herself along with his or her interlocutors. Indeed, we are in the process

[1] http://code.google.com/p/aiml-en-us-foundation-alice/, retrieved February 2012.

```
PREV      okay .
ACTUAL    okay .
ALICE     Great.

PREV      please don't leave .
ACTUAL    i'm right here .
ALICE     I'm not going anywhere.
```

```
PREV      you need to drink water .
ACTUAL    no , stay .
ALICE     I need to wait and see if the
          opportunity presents itself.

PREV      okay ?
ACTUAL    you were so mad at me
          lately , dixie .
ALICE     Dude!
```

Figure 3: Some responses generated by ALICE.

of collecting a corpus of such interactions from a small number of AAC users in the Portland, Oregon area. But the resulting corpora will obviously be tiny in comparison with the data used in the experiments here, in no small measure because of the extreme slowness with which most AAC users are able to communicate. What can be done about this? One thing would be to use the results of this work directly even if it does not model the particular user: even if it comes from soap opera dialogs, *Are you mad at me? No, I'm not mad at you*, still makes for a perfectly reasonable utterance/response pair. This, to some extent, counters potential objections that soap opera dialogs are not reflective of natural interactions. These kinds of pairs could be supplemented by whatever data we are able to learn from a particular user.

Even better, though, would be to collect large amounts of data from users *before* they become impaired. Many disorders, such as ALS, are often detected early, before they start to impair communication. In such cases, one could consider language-banking the user's interactions, and building a model of the ways in which the user interacts with other speakers, in order to get a good model of that *particular* user. While there are obviously privacy concerns, a person who knows that they will lose the ability to speak over time will likely be very motivated to try to preserve samples of their speech and language, assuming there exists technology that can use those samples to provide more sophisticated assistance when it becomes needed.

It may also be possible to use features from the text to generate utterances, similar to the telegraphic approaches to generation discussed in Section 2, but automatically learning words that can be used to generate appropriate responses to an utterance. As a first look at the feasibility of this approach, we use the Midge generator (Mitchell et al., 2012), rebuilding its models from the soap dialogues. Midge requires as input a set of nouns and then builds likely syntactic structure around them, and so we use the dialogues to predict possible nouns in response to an input utterance. For each <utterance, response> pair in the dialogues, we gather all utterance nouns n_u and all response nouns n_r. We then compute normalized pointwise mutual information (nPMI) for each n_u, n_r pair type in the corpus. Given a novel input utterance, we tag it to extract the nouns and create the set of highest nPMI nouns from the model. This is then input to Midge, which uses the set to generate present-tense declarative sentences. Some examples are given in Figure 4. We hope to expand on this approach in future work.

A further improvement is to take advantage of synonymy. There are many ways to convey the same basic message: *i am sick*, *i am not feeling well*, *i'm under the weather*, are all ways for a speaker to convey that he or she is not in the best of health. In the current system, these are all treated separately. Clearly what is needed is a way of recognizing that these are all *paraphrases* of each other. Fortunately, there has been a lot of progress in recent years on paraphrasing — see Ganitkevitch et al. (2011) for a recent example — and such work could in principle be adapted to the problem here. Indeed it seems likely that incorporating paraphrasing into the system will be a *major* source of improved coverage.

A limitation of the work described here is that it only models turn-to-turn interactions. Clearly discourse models need to have more memory than this, so features that relate to earlier turns would be needed. The downside is that this would quickly lead to data sparsity.

There are a variety of machine learning techniques that could also be tried, beyond the rather

Input: `this is n't the same . this is not like anything i have been through before . i mean , how am i supposed to make it work with somebody who ...`
Pred. nouns: `strength, somebody`
Output: `strength comes with somebody`

Input: `i 've been a little bit too busy to socialize . i did have an interesting conversation with your sister , however .`
Pred. nouns: `bit, conversation, sister`
Output: `a bit about this conversation with sister`

Figure 4: Generating with nPMI: Creating syntactic structure around likely nouns.

simple methods employed in this work. For example, particular classes of response types, comprising a variety of related utterances, may be predictable using the extracted features.

Finally, we have assumed for this discussion that the AAC system is only within the control of the impaired user. There is no reason to make that assumption in general: many AAC situations in real life involve a helper who will often *co-construct* with the impaired user. Such helpers usually know the impaired user very well and can often make reasonable guesses as to the whole utterance intended by the impaired user. Recent work reported in Roark et al. (2011) suggests one way in which the results of a language modeling system and those of a human co-constructor may be integrated into a single system, and such an approach could easily be applied here.

7 Conclusions

We have proposed and evaluated an approach to whole utterance prediction for AAC. While the approach is fairly simple, it is able to generate correct or at least reasonable responses in some cases. Such a system could be used in conjunction with other techniques, such as language-model-based prediction, or co-construction. One of the potentially useful side-effects of this work is an estimate of what percentage of interactions in a dialog are likely to be easily handled by such techniques. In other words, how many interactions in dialog are sufficiently predictable that a system could have a reasonable guess as to what a speaker is going to say given the previous context? A rough estimate based on what we have found here is something on the order of 3.5%-4.0%. Obviously this does not mean that the system will always make the right prediction: a reasonable response to *congratulations on your promotion* would often be *thank you*, but a speaker may wish to say something else. But what it does mean is that in about 3.5%-4.0% of cases, one has a reasonable chance of being able to guess. This percentage is certainly small, and one might be inclined to conclude that the approach does not work. On the other hand, it is important to bear in mind that not all percentages are created equal. Rapid responses to basic phrases (e.g. *Are you mad at me?* → *No, I'm not mad at you*), could help with the perceived flow of conversation, even if they do not occur that frequently.

As we noted at the outset, whole utterance prediction is an area that has received increased interest in recent years, because of its potential to speed communication, and its contribution to increasing the naturalness of conversational interactions. When coupled with gains in utterance generation achieved by other methods, automatically generating utterances can further the range of comments and responses available to AAC users. The work reported here is a small contribution towards this goal.

Acknowledgments

This work was supported under grant NIH-K25DC011308. Sproat thanks his K25 mentor, Melanie Fried-Oken, for discussion and support. We also thank four anonymous reviewers, as well as the audience at a Center for Spoken Language Understanding seminar, for their comments.

References

N. Alm, J. L. Arnott, and A. F. Newell. 1992. Prediction and conversational momentum in an augmentative communication system. *Communications of the ACM*, 35(5):46–57.

N. Alm, J. Todman, Leona Elder, and A. F. Newell. 1993. Computer aided conversation for severely physically impaired non-speaking people. *Proceedings of INTERCHI '93*, pages 236–241.

Bruce Baker. 1990. Semantic compaction: a basic technology for artificial intelligence in AAC. In *5th Annual Minspeak Conference*.

J. J. Darragh, I. H. Witten, and M. L. James. 1990. The reactive keyboard: A predictive typing aid. *Computer*, 23(11):41–49.

Martin Dempster, Norman Alm, and Ehud Reiter. 2010. Automatic generation of conversational utterances and narrative for augmentative and alternative communication: A prototype system. *Proceedings of the Workshop on Speech and Language Processing for Assistive Technologies (SLPAT)*, pages 10–18.

R. Dye, N. Alm, J. L. Arnott, G. Harper, and A Morrison. 1998. A script-based AAC system for transactional interaction. *Natural Language Engineering*, 4(1):57–71.

Michael Elhadad. 1991. FUF: The universal unifer-user manual version 5.0. Technical report.

Jenny Rose Finkel, Trond Grenager, and Christopher Manning. 2005. Incorporating non-local information into information extraction systems by gibbs sampling. *Proceedings of the 43rd Annual Meeting of the Association for Computational Linguistics (ACL)*, pages 363–370.

Juri Ganitkevitch, Chris Callison-Burch, Courtney Napoles, and Benjamin van Durme. 2011. Learning sentential paraphrases from bilingual parallel corpora for text-to-text generation. *Proceedings of Empirical Methods in Natural Language Processing (EMNLP)*.

John Godfrey and Edward Holliman. 1997. Switchboard-1 release 2. Linguistic Data Consortium, Philadelphia.

D. J. Higginbotham, D. P. Wilkins, G. W. Lesher, and B. J. Moulton. 1999. Frametalker: A communication frame and utterance-based augmentative communication device. Technical Report.

D. Jeffery Higginbotham. 1992. Evaluation of keystroke savings across five assistive communication technologies. *Augmentative and Alternative Communication*, 8:258–272.

Julia King, Tracie Spoeneman, Sheela Stuart, and David Beukelman. 1995. Small talk in adult conversations: Implications for AAC vocabulary selection. *Augmentative and Alternative Communication*, 11:260–264.

Dan Klein and Christopher D. Manning. 2003. Accurate unlexicalized parsing. *Proceedings of the 41st Meeting of the Association for Computational Linguistics (ACL)*, pages 423–430.

S. Langer and M. Hickey. 1998. Using semantic lexicons for full text message retrieval in a communication aid. *Natural Language Engineering*, 4(1):41–55.

Heeyoung Lee, Yves Peirsman, Angel Chang, Nathanael Chambers, Mihai Surdeanu, and Dan Jurafsky. 2011. Stanford's multi-pass sieve coreference resolution system at the conll-2011 shared task. *Proceedings of the CoNLL-2011 Shared Task*.

J. Li and G. Hirst. 2005. Semantic knowledge in word completion. In *Proceedings of the 7th International ACM Conference on Computers and Accessibility*.

K. McCoy, C. A. Pennington, and A. L. Badman. 1998. Compansion: From research prototype to practical integration. *Natural Language Engineering*, 4(1):73–95.

Kathleen F. McCoy, Jan L. Bedrosian, Linda A. Hoag, and Dallas E. Johnson. 2007. Brevity and speed of message delivery trade-offs in augmentative and alternative communication. *Augmentative and Alternative Communication*, 23(1):76–88.

Margaret Mitchell, Jesse Dodge, Amit Goyal, Kota Yamaguchi, Karl Sratos, Xufeng Han, Alysssa Mensch, Alex Berg, Tamara L. Berg, and Hal Daumé III. 2012. Midge: Generating image descriptions from computer vision detections. *Proceedings of EACL 2012*.

Y. Netzer and M. Elhadad. 2006. Using semantic authoring for Blissymbols communication boards. *Proceedings of HLT 2006*, pages 105–108.

Amruta Purandare and Diane Litman. 2008. Analyzing dialog coherence using transition patterns in lexical and semantic features. In *FLAIRS Conference*, pages 195–200.

Brian Roark, Andrew Fowler, Richard Sproat, Christopher Gibbons, and Melanie Fried-Oken. 2011. Towards technology-assisted co-construction with communication partners. *Proceedings of the Workshop on Speech and Language Processing for Assistive Technologies (SLPAT)*.

Cort Stratton. 2010. PyAIML, a Python AIML interpreter. http://pyaiml.sourceforge.net/.

J. Todman, A. Norman, J. Higginbotham, and P. File. 2008. Whole utterance approaches in AAC. *Augmentative and Alternative Communication*, 24(3):235–254.

Kristina Toutanova, Dan Klein, Christopher Manning, and Yoram Singer. 2003. Feature-rich part-of-speech tagging with a cyclic dependency network. *Proceedings of HLT-NAACL*, pages 252–259.

K. Trnka, D. Yarrington, K.F. McCoy, and C. Pennington. 2006. Topic modeling in fringe word prediction for AAC. In *Proceedings of the International Conference on Intelligent User Interfaces*, pages 276–278.

K. Trnka, D. Yarrington, J. McCaw, K.F. McCoy, and C. Pennington. 2007. The effects of word prediction on communication rate for AAC. In *Proceedings of HLT-NAACL; Companion Volume, Short Papers*, pages 173–176.

H. Trost, J. Matiasek, and M. Baroni. 2005. The language component of the FASTY text prediction system. *Applied Artificial Intelligence*, 19(8):743–781.

Richard Wallace. 2012. A.L.I.C.E. (Artificial Linguistic Internet Computer Entity). http://www.alicebot.org/.

T. Wandmacher and J.Y. Antoine. 2007. Methods to integrate a language model with semantic information for a word prediction component. In *Proceedings of Empirical Methods in Natural Language Processing (EMNLP)*, pages 506–513.

Joseph Weizenbaum. 1966. Eliza – a computer program for the study of natural language communication between man and machine. *Proceedings of the ACM*, 9(1).

Bruce Wisenburn and D. Jeffery Higginbotham. 2008. An AAC application using speaking partner speech recognition to automatically produce contextually relevant utterances: Objective results. *Augmentative and Alternative Communication*, 24(2):100–109.

Applying Prediction Techniques to Phoneme-based AAC Systems

Keith Vertanen
Department of Computer Science
Montana Tech of the University of Montana
keithv@keithv.com

Ha Trinh, Annalu Waller, Vicki L. Hanson
School of Computing
University of Dundee
{hatrinh, awaller, vlh}
@computing.dundee.ac.uk

Per Ola Kristensson
School of Computer Science
University of St Andrews
pok@st-andrews.ac.uk

Abstract

It is well documented that people with severe speech and physical impairments (SSPI) often experience literacy difficulties, which hinder them from effectively using orthographic-based AAC systems for communication. To address this problem, phoneme-based AAC systems have been proposed, which enable users to access a set of spoken phonemes and combine phonemes into speech output. In this paper we investigate how prediction techniques can be applied to improve user performance of such systems. We have developed a phoneme-based prediction system, which supports single phoneme prediction and phoneme-based word prediction using statistical language models generated using a crowdsourced AAC-like corpus. We incorporated our prediction system into a hypothetical 12-key reduced phoneme keyboard. A computational experiment showed that our prediction system led to 56.3% average keystroke savings.

1 Introduction

Over the last forty years there has been an increasing number of high-tech AAC systems developed to provide communication support for individuals with severe speech and physical impairments (SSPI). Most of existing AAC systems can be classified into two categories, namely graphic-based and orthographic-based systems. Graphic-based systems utilize symbols to encode a limited set of frequently used words and utterances, thereby supporting fast access to pre-stored items. However, there is a high cognitive overhead associated with learning the encoding methods of these systems, which can be problematic for many AAC users, especially those with intellectual disabilities. In addition, users of these systems are limited to pre-programmed items rather than being able to create novel words and messages spontaneously. In contrast, orthographic-based AAC systems allow users to spell out their own messages. Prediction techniques, such as character or word prediction, are often applied to improve the usability and accessibility of these systems. However, these systems require users to master literacy skills, a well-documented problem for many children and adults with SSPI (Koppenhaver and Yoder, 1992).

The question arises as to how AAC systems can be designed to enable pre-literate users with SSPI to generate novel words and messages in spontaneous conversations. A potential solution for this question is to adopt a phoneme-to-speech generation approach. This approach allows users to access a limited set of spoken phonemes and blend phonemes into speech output, thereby enabling them to create spontaneous messages without knowledge of orthographic spelling. This approach has been applied in several phoneme-based AAC systems to support communication (Glennen and DeCoste, 1997) and literacy learning (Black et al., 2008). It has also been utilized as an alternative typing method for people with spelling difficulties (Schroeder, 2005).

Despite such potential, phoneme-based AAC systems have been an under-researched topic. In particular, little work has been done on the application of Natural Language Processing (NLP) techniques to these systems. Thus, in this paper we investigate how prediction methods can be incorporated into phoneme-based AAC systems to facilitate phoneme entry. We develop a basic phoneme-based prediction system, which provides predictions at both phoneme and word levels based on statistical language modeling techniques. We use a 6-gram phoneme mixture model and a 3-gram word mixture model trained on a large set of AAC-like data assembled from multiple sources, such as Twitter, Blog, and Usenet data. We take into consideration issues such as pronunciation variants and user accents in the design of our system. We performed a theoretical evaluation of our system on three different test sets using a simulated interface and report results of hit rate and potential keystroke savings. Finally, we propose a number of further studies to extend the current work.

2 Background

2.1 Phoneme-based AAC Systems

The idea of using phonemes in AAC systems was first commercially introduced by Phonic Ear in 1978 in the HandiVoice 110 (Creech, 2004; Glennen and DeCoste, 1997; Williams, 1995). The device provided users with direct access to a mixed vocabulary consisting of pre-programmed words, short phrases, letters, morphemes, and 45 phonemes. Users could generate synthetic speech from phoneme sequences using the Votrax speech synthesizer. Similar to the HandiVoice is the Finger Foniks, a handheld communicator developed by Words+ (Glennen and DeCoste, 1997). The device enables users to access prerecorded messages and a set of 36 phonemes from which they could generate unlimited speech output. Neither of these devices offered any prediction features.

The PhonicStick™, a talking joystick (Black et al., 2008), is a phoneme-based AAC device developed by researchers at the University of Dundee. Unlike the HandiVoice and the Finger Foniks, the primary use of the PhonicStick™ is to facilitate language play and phonics teaching for children with SSPI. The device allows users to access the 42 phonemes used in the Jolly Phonics literacy program (Lloyd, 1998) by moving the joystick along pre-defined paths. A prototype of the PhonicStick™, using a subset of 6 Jolly Phonics' phonemes, has been evaluated with seven children without and with SSPI. Results of the evaluations demonstrated that the participants could create short words using the phonemes. However, some participants with poor hand function experienced significant difficulties in using the joystick to select target phonemes (Black et al., 2008). This suggests that the PhonicStick™ could benefit from prediction mechanisms to reduce the number of difficult joystick movements required for each phoneme entry.

The phoneme-to-speech approach is not only applied in dedicated AAC systems but also in alternative typing interfaces for individuals with spelling difficulties. An example of such applications is the REACH Sound-It-Out Phonetic Keyboard™ (Schroeder, 2005). This on-screen keyboard comprises 40 phonemes and 4 phoneme combinations. It offers two types of prediction features, including phoneme prediction and word prediction. The phoneme prediction feature uses a pronunciation dictionary to determine which phonemes cannot follow the currently selected phonemes. These phonemes are then removed from the keyboard, thereby facilitating users in visually scanning and identifying the next phoneme in the intended word. The word prediction feature also uses a dictionary to search for the most frequently used words that phonetically match the currently selected phoneme sequence. To our knowledge, this is the only currently available system that provides phoneme-based predictions. However, these predictions use a simple dictionary-based prediction algorithm, which does not take into account contextual information (e.g. prior text). There has been little or no published research into how more advanced NLP techniques can be employed to improve the performance of phoneme-based predictions.

2.2 Prediction in AAC Systems

Prediction techniques have been extensively utilized in many AAC systems to achieve keystroke savings and potential communication rate enhancement (Garay-Victoria and Abascal, 2005). There are various prediction strategies that have been developed in these systems, of which the most commonly used are character prediction and word prediction. Character prediction anticipates next probable characters given the preceding characters. It is typically applied in reduced keyboards and scanning-based AAC systems to augment the scanning process (Lesher et al., 1998). Word prediction anticipates the word being entered on the basis of the previously selected characters and words, thereby saving the user the effort of entering every character of a word.

Most existing prediction systems employ statistical language modelling techniques to perform prediction tasks. Prediction accuracy generally increases with higher-order n-gram language models. However, most systems are limited to 6-gram models for character prediction and 3-gram models for word prediction, as the gain from higher-order models is often small at the cost of considerably increased computational and storage resources. To further improve the prediction performance, a number of advanced language modelling techniques have been investigated, which take into account additional information such as word recency (Swiffin et al., 1987), syntactic information (Hunnicutt and Caarlberger, 2001; Swiffin et al., 1987), semantic information (Li and Hirst, 2005), and topic modelling (Trnka et al., 2006). These techniques have the potential of improved keystroke savings at the cost of increased computational complexity.

A fundamental issue of the statistical-based prediction approach is that its performance is heavily dependent on the size of the training corpus and the degree to which the corpus represents the domain of use. Therefore, in the development of statistical-based prediction for conversational AAC systems, it may be ideal to construct language models from a large corpus of transcribed conversations of real AAC users. However, such a corpus has been unavailable to date. To address this problem, previous research has utilized corpora of telephone transcripts, such as the Switchboard corpus, and performed cleanup processing to make them a more appropriate approximate of AAC communication (Lesher and Rinkus, 2002; Trnka et al., 2006). Vertanen and Kristensson (2011) have recently proposed a novel solution to this problem by creating a large corpus of fictional AAC messages. Using Amazon Mechanical Market, the researchers crowdsourced a small dataset of AAC-like messages, which was then used to select a much larger set of AAC-like data from Twitter, Blog, and Usenet datasets. The language models trained on this AAC-like corpus were proved to outperform other models trained on telephone transcripts (Vertanen and Kristensson, 2011).

3 Phoneme-based Prediction System

Although statistical-based predictions have been a well-studied topic, little or no research has been published on how well these predictions can be adapted to phoneme-based AAC systems. In this section, we describe our phoneme-based prediction system, which employs statistical language modeling techniques to perform phoneme prediction and phoneme-based word prediction. Phoneme prediction predicts probable next phonemes based on the previously entered phonemes. Word prediction predicts the word currently being entered based on the current phoneme prefix and prior words.

3.1 Phoneme Set

Unlike traditional orthographic-based AAC systems that operate on a standard character set, different phoneme-based systems tend to use slightly different phoneme sets. For our prediction system, we use the phoneme set from the Jolly Phonics, a systematic synthetic phonics program widely used in the UK for literacy teaching (Lloyd, 1998). The phoneme set, to be called the PHONICS set, consists of 42 phonemes, with 17 vowels and 25 consonants. By using a literacy-linked phoneme set, our prediction system can readily be integrated into both literacy learning tools (such as the PhonicStick™ joystick (Black et al., 2008)) and communication aids. Other systems that use different phoneme sets can also be easily adapted to utilize our prediction system by providing a phoneme mapping scheme between their phoneme sets and the PHONICS set.

3.2 Pronunciation Dictionary

3.2.1 The PHONICS Dictionary

The development of phoneme-based predictions requires a pronunciation dictionary, which should be accent-specific as pronunciations may vary across different accents. There has been no dictionary to date that contains word pronunciations using the PHONICS set. To address this problem, we built our PHONICS pronunciation dictionary based on the Unisyn[1] lexicon, as it provides facilities for generating dictionaries in different accents. The Unisyn uses the concept of key-symbols (i.e. meta-phonemes) to encode the characteristics of

[1] http://www.cstr.ed.ac.uk/projects/unisyn/

[2] http://aac.unl.edu/vocabulary.html, accessed 4 September

multiple accents into a single base lexicon. Accent-specific rules can then be applied to the base lexicon to produce pronunciations in a given accent.

To create the PHONICS dictionary, we first derived a lexicon in the Edinburgh accent from the base lexicon using a set of Perl scripts supplied with Unisyn. We also performed additional clean-up processing to remove unwanted information, such as stress and boundary markers. We then created a mapping function from the set of 61 phonemes and allophones used in the Edinburgh lexicon to the PHONICS set. As the PHONICS set only contains 42 phonemes, several allophones in the Edinburgh set were mapped to the same phonemes in the PHONICS set. This mapping function was then used to convert the Edinburgh lexicon to the PHONICS pronunciation dictionary. The resulting dictionary consists of 121,004 pronunciation entries for 117,625 unique words.

3.2.2 The Schwa Phoneme

An issue of the phoneme mapping is that the Edinburgh set contains the schwa phoneme (denoted by the symbol '@'), which cannot be mapped to any phonemes in the PHONICS set. The schwa, a reduced form of full vowels in unstressed syllables, occurs in 41,539 entries in the PHONICS dictionary. An example of a word containing the schwa phoneme is *'today' (/t @ d ai/).* While the schwa is the most commonly used vowel sound in spoken English (Gimson and Cruttenden, 2001), it is not included in the Jolly Phonics teaching as it is a difficult concept to understand for literacy learners at early stages.

The simplest solution for this issue would be to explicitly add the schwa phoneme into the PHONICS set in our prediction system. However, learning to use the schwa correctly can be challenging for users with SSPI and literacy difficulties. Thus, we decided to support two modes in our system, namely the SCHWA_ON and the SCHWA_OFF modes. In the SCHWA_ON mode, the schwa phoneme is explicitly added to the PHONICS set, increasing the set to 43 phonemes. In the SCHWA_OFF mode, the schwa is not added into the PHONICS set and therefore is not offered to the users for selection. To deal with the absence of the schwa, we employed a basic auto-correction method. To search for a word given a phoneme sequence, we apply a limited set of schwa insertion and replacement rules (e.g. replacing vowels with schwas) to generate a set of alternative sequences. These sequences and the original sequence are then used to look up a list of matching words in the PHONICS dictionary. Once the user has selected a word from this list, the correct pronunciation of the selected word (which might include the schwas) would be used to replace the original phoneme sequence in the currently selected phoneme string. This corrected phoneme string would then be input to the phoneme language model (described in Section 3.3.1) to predict probable next phonemes.

3.3 Phoneme Prediction

We trained a 6-gram phoneme language model starting with training data from:

- Twitter messages collected via the free streaming API between December 2010 and July 2011. 36M sentences, 251M words.
- Blog posts from the ICWSM corpus (Burton et al., 2009). 25M sentences, 387M words.
- Usenet messages (Shaoul and Westbury, 2009). 123M sentences, 1847M words.

We used the crowdsourced data from Vertanen and Kristensson (2011) to select AAC-like sentences using cross-entropy difference selection (Moore and Lewis, 2010). The selection process retained 6.9M, 1.6M, and 2.3M words of data from the Twitter, Blog and Usenet data sets respectively. We converted the words in the selected sentences to pronunciation strings using the PHONICS dictionary. Whenever we encountered a word with multiple pronunciations, we chose a pronunciation at random. If a sentence had a word not in the PHONICS dictionary, we dropped the entire training sentence.

We trained a 6-gram phoneme language model for each of the Twitter, Blog, and Usenet data sets. Estimation of unigrams used Witten-Bell discounting while all higher order n-grams used modified Kneser-Ney discounting with interpolation. We then created a mixture model via linear interpolation with mixture weights optimized on the crowdsourced development set from Vertanen and Kristensson (2011). The optimized mixture weights were: Twitter 0.54, Blog 0.25, and Usenet 0.21. Our final mixture model has 2.0M parameters and a compressed disk size of 14 MB.

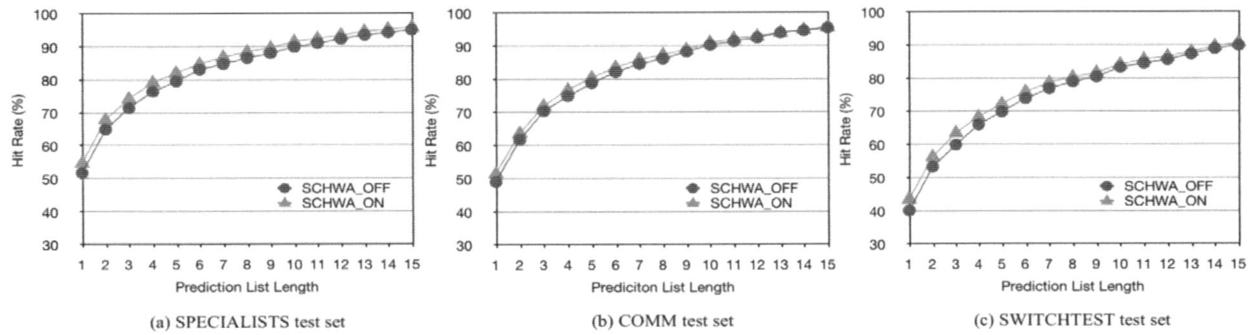

Figure 1. Hit rates of the phoneme prediction for prediction list lengths 1-15 in the SWCHA_ON and SCHWA_OFF modes. Results on the SPECIALISTS, COMM, and SWITCHTEST test sets.

3.3.1 Hit Rate

We evaluated the accuracy of our phoneme prediction using hit rate. Hit rate (HR) is defined as the percentage of times that the intended phonemes appear in the prediction list:

$$HR = \frac{\text{Number of times the phoneme is predicted}}{\text{Number of phonemes}} \times 100\%$$

We computed the hit rates for prediction lists of lengths 1-15 in both SCHWA_ON and SCHWA_OFF modes. The results of this evaluation would help inform the decision of the number of predicted items to be presented to the users, which is a key usability factor of prediction systems.

We evaluated the hit rates on the following test sets:

- SPECIALISTS: A collection of context specific conversational phrases recommended by AAC professionals[2]. 966 sentences, 3814 words. Out-of-vocabulary (OOV) rate: 0.05%.
- COMM: A collection of sentences written by college students in response to 10 hypothetical communication situations (Venkatagiri, 1999). 251 sentences, 1789 words. OOV rate: 0.3%.
- SWITCHTEST: Three telephone transcripts taken from the Switchboard corpus, used in Trnka et al. (2009). 59 sentences, 508 words. OOV rate: 0.4%.

These three test sets are used throughout this paper. For each sentence in the test sets, we generated its pronunciation string using the PHONICS dictionary. During this generation, any time we encountered a word with multiple pronunciations, we chose a pronunciation at random. We manually added pronunciations for OOV words. The generated pronunciations were used to calculate the hit rates in the SCHWA_ON mode. We then created a 'non-schwa' version of each pronunciation string, in which we removed all schwa occurrences by either deleting them or replacing them with appropriate vowels in the PHONICS set. The 'non-schwa' pronunciations were used to calculate the hit rates in the SCHWA_OFF mode.

As shown in Figure 1, the hit rate improved as the prediction list length (L) increased in both the SCHWA_OFF and SCHWA_ON modes for all the three test sets. For most L values, the system performed the best on the SPECIALISTS test set and the worst on the SWITCHTEST set. At L=1, the average hit rates for the three test sets were 47.1% in the SCHWA_OFF mode and 50.1% in the SWITCH_ON mode. At L=5 (which is the length usually offered in prediction systems), the average hit rate increased to 76.2% in the SCHWA_OFF mode and 78.4% in the SCHWA_ON mode. At L=15, the system reached high average hit rates of 93.6% in the SCHWA_OFF mode and 94.3% in the SCHWA_ON mode.

The SCHWA_ON mode achieved higher hit rates than the SCHWA_OFF mode for all L values. However, the hit rate differences between these two modes tended to diminish as L increased. At L=1, the average difference for the three test sets was 3.0%. At L=5, the average difference reduced to 2.2%. At L=15, the average difference was very small, at 0.7%.

[2] http://aac.unl.edu/vocabulary.html, accessed 4 September 2011

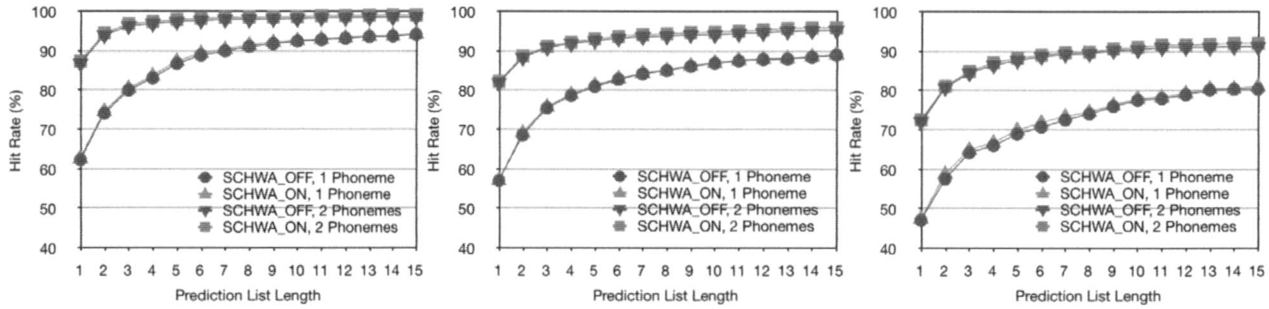

(a) SPECIALISTS test set (b) COMM test set (c) SWITCHTEST test set

Figure 2. Hit rates of the word prediction for prediction list lengths 1-15 in the SWCHA_ON and SCHWA_OFF modes for 1-phoneme and 2-phoneme prefixes. Results on the SPECIALISTS, COMM, and SWITCHTEST test sets.

3.4 Phoneme-based Word Prediction

We used a publicly available 3-gram word mixture model[3], which was created from three 3-gram models trained on AAC-like data from Twitter, Blog, and Usenet (Vertanen and Kristensson, 2011). Although a 4-gram model trained on the same datasets is also available, it was not used in our system as it has been shown to only slightly outperform the 3-gram model at the cost of a much bigger model size (Vertanen and Kristensson, 2011). Our aim is to keep our prediction system's size reasonably small, thereby allowing it to be easily integrated into devices with limited resources, such as mobile devices.

To perform word prediction given a phoneme prefix, we first search for a set of matching words in the PHONICS dictionary. In the SCHWA_OFF mode, the phoneme prefix is input to the auto-correction function to generate alternative prefixes, which are then used to look up matching words in the dictionary. If there is no matching word, an unknown word (denoted as <unk>) is returned. The matching words are then input to the word model to calculate their probabilities based on up to two prior words.

3.4.1 Hit Rate

We computed the hit rate (HR) of word prediction for prediction list lengths 1-15 in two conditions: (1) after the first phoneme is entered, (2) after the first two phonemes are entered:

$$\mathrm{HR} = \frac{\text{Number of times the word is predicted}}{\text{Number of words}} \times 100\%$$

Figure 2 shows the hit rates of word prediction in the SCHWA_OFF and SCHWA_ON modes on the three test sets. As expected, the hit rates improved as the prediction list length (L) increased. Table 1 summarizes the average hit rates for several list lengths for 1-phoneme and 2-phoneme prefixes. At L=5, the average hit rates were 92.5% in the SCHWA_OFF mode and 93.2% in the SCHWA_ON mode after the first two phonemes are entered. This means that in most cases, the intended word is predicted after two keystrokes. The SCHWA_ON mode achieved higher hit rates than the SCHWA_OFF mode in all cases. However, the hit rate differences between these two modes were very small (<1%), which implies that our auto-correction mechanism was effective.

L	SCHWA_OFF		SCHWA_ON	
	1-phoneme	2-phoneme	1-phoneme	2-phoneme
1	55.6%	80.4%	55.9%	80.8%
5	79.0%	92.5%	79.7%	93.2%
10	86.0%	94.5%	86.2%	95.0%
15	88.0%	95.1%	88.3%	95.8%

Table 1. Average hit rates of word prediction.

4 Theoretical Evaluation

AAC users with physical impairments often experience difficulties in accessing a large number of keys on conventional full-sized keyboards. To address this problem, previous research has proposed the use of reduced keyboards (i.e. keyboards on which each key is assigned a group of charac-

3 http://www.aactext.org/imagine/lm_mix_top3_3gram_abs0.0.arpa.gz

ters, such as the 12-key mobile phone keyboard) (Arnott and Javed, 1992; Kushler, 1998). Character prediction and word prediction can be applied to these keyboards to disambiguate characters on each key. We adopted this idea by creating a hypothetical 12-key phoneme keyboard and evaluated the benefits of incorporating phoneme prediction and word prediction into the keyboard.

4.1 Phoneme-based Predictive Interface

Our 12-key phoneme keyboard contains 8 phoneme keys, which represent 3 vowel groups and 5 consonant groups. These groups, introduced in the PhonicStick™ talking joystick (Black et al., 2008; Lindström and Peronius, 2010), are formed according to the manner of articulation of the phonemes (see Figure 3a). Each key represents three to seven phonemes; the schwa phoneme is excluded. The phonemes on each key are initially arranged according to the unigram probabilities estimated by our phoneme language model.

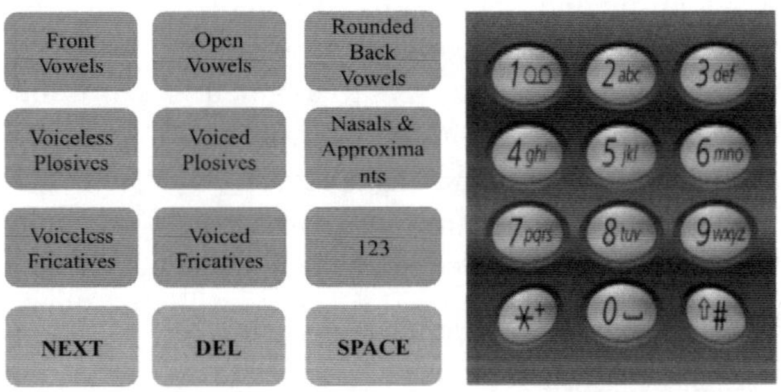

a. The 12-key phoneme keyboard b. The standard 12-key mobile phone keyboard

Figure 3. Phoneme-based reduced keyboard.

The keyboard provides two phoneme entry modes, namely the MULTITAP and the PREDICTIVE modes. In the MULTITAP mode, the user enters a phoneme by pressing a corresponding key repeatedly until the intended phoneme appears (e.g. pressing the 'Unvoiced Plosives' key 3 times to enter /p/). In the PREDICTIVE mode, the keyboard utilizes our prediction system in its SCHWA_OFF mode to predict probable next phonemes and words. Each time the user presses a key the phoneme prediction is applied to guess which of the possible phonemes on the pressed key is actually the user's intended phoneme. If the prediction is incorrect, the user can repeatedly press the NEXT key until the correct phoneme is selected. After each phoneme selection, we present a list of up to 5 predicted words. We only offer word predictions after the first phoneme of a new word is entered. If the intended word appears in the prediction list, we assume it takes one keystroke for the user to add the word and a following space to the current sentence (this can be implemented using automatic scanning (Glennen and DeCoste, 1997)).

4.2 Results

We evaluated our prediction system using two commonly used metrics: keystroke savings and keystrokes per character.

4.2.1 Keystroke Savings

Keystroke Savings (KS) is defined as the percentage of keystrokes that the user saves by using prediction methods compared to using the MULTITAP method:

$$KS = \left(1 - \frac{Keystrokes_{PREDICTION}}{Keystrokes_{MULTITAP}}\right) \times 100\%$$

We computed KS on the three test sets for three methods: (1) only phoneme prediction (PP), (2) only word prediction (WP), (3) combined phoneme prediction and word prediction (PP+WP) (i.e. the PREDICTIVE mode).

As shown in Figure 4, a combined phoneme and word prediction method performed the best with an average keystroke savings of 56.3%. Using only word prediction led to a 46.4% average KS while using only phoneme prediction resulted in 29.9% average KS.

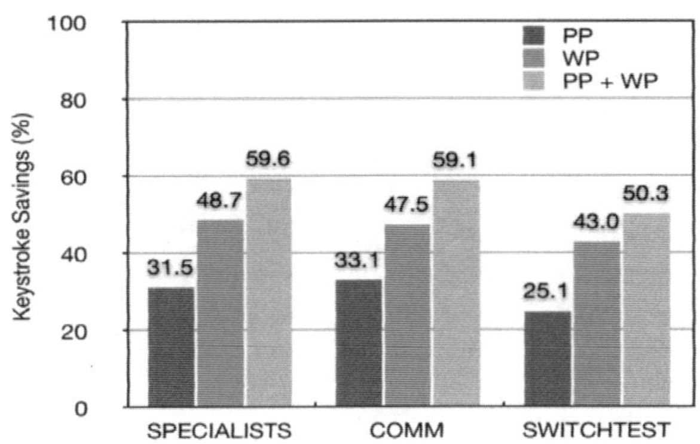

Figure 4. Keystroke Savings (KS) for prediction methods on three test sets.

4.2.2 Keystrokes Per Character

Keystrokes per character (KSPC) is defined as the average number of keystrokes required to produce a character in the test set:

$$\text{KSPC} = \frac{\text{Keystrokes}}{\text{Number of characters (including spaces)}}$$

The evaluation of KSPC allows us to compare our keyboard with existing character-based reduced keyboards. We computed the KSPC for four methods: (1) MULTITAP, (2) PP, (3) WP, (4) PP+WP. For comparison, we also calculated the KSPC for a standard 12-key mobile phone alphabetic keyboard (Figure 3b), which uses the character-based multitap method for text entry.

As shown in Figure 5, our frequency-based phoneme keyboard outperformed the standard mobile phone keyboard even when no prediction methods are applied (i.e. in the MULTITAP mode) (see Figure 5). At an average KSPC of 1.568, our keyboard required 19.1% fewer keystrokes per character than the mobile phone multitap keyboard (KSPC=1.937). There are two reasons that might explain this result. First, on average one phoneme represents more than one character (in our dictionary, the character/phoneme ratio is 1.208). Second, our keyboard's phonemes were initially ordered by the unigram frequencies.

When applying only phoneme prediction, the average KSPC decreased to 1.100, which closely approaches the KSPC of a QWERTY keyboard (KSPC=1). The KSPC further reduced to 0.841 with solely word prediction and 0.685 with combined phoneme and word prediction.

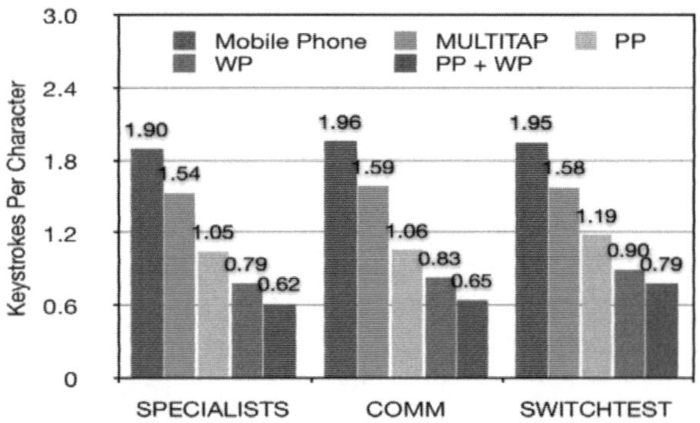

Figure 5. Keystrokes Per Character (KSPC) for different text entry methods on three test sets.

5 Conclusions and Future Work

In this paper we have described how statistical language modeling techniques can be used to provide phoneme prediction and word prediction for phoneme-based AAC systems. Using hit rate measurement we demonstrated how the prediction accuracy improved as the prediction list length increased. However, a large prediction list might result in an increased time and cognitive workload required from the user to scan the list and select the desired item. Therefore, hit rate data need to be combined with empirical experiments with real users in order to determine an appropriate prediction list length.

We evaluated our prediction system on a 12-key phoneme keyboard, in which phonemes are grouped based on the manner of articulation and ordered using our phoneme unigram frequencies. We showed that we could achieve a potential keystroke savings of 56.3% by applying a combined phoneme and word prediction to our keyboard. Using word prediction alone proved to be more effective than using phoneme prediction alone, in terms of keystroke savings.

We plan to take this work forward by exploring two complementary research directions.

First, we plan to conduct empirical experiments with a group of AAC users to evaluate the usability of our phoneme predictive keyboard. We are interested in finding out if the potential keystroke savings can be translated into an actual keystroke savings and communication rate enhancement. In addition, we will analyze user's errors in phoneme selection, which can be used to produce a more advanced auto-correction method.

Second, we will explore how our prediction system can be integrated into existing phoneme-based AAC systems rather than our reduced keyboard. In particular, we will focus on the REACH Sound-It-Out Phonetic Keyboard™ (Schroeder, 2005), which uses a different phoneme set than our PHONICS set, and the PhonicStick™ (Black et al., 2008), which has the same phoneme groupings as our keyboard.

Finally, we will investigate how NLP techniques, such as the joint-multigram model (Bisani and Ney, 2008), can be applied to automatically generate orthographic spellings for OOV words. Our current system simply uses a <unk> placeholder for OOV words. While these words can still be spoken out by synthesizing their phoneme strings, it is potentially more beneficial to suggest actual spellings than to use such a placeholder.

References

John L. Arnott and Muhammad Y. Javed (1992). Probabilistic character disambiguation for reduced keyboard using small text samples. *Augmentative and Alternative Communication, 8*(3), 215-223.

Maximilian Bisani and Hermann Ney (2008). Joint-sequence models for grapheme-to-phoneme conversion. *Speech Communication, 50*(5), 434-451.

Rolf Black, Annalu Waller, Graham Pullin, and Eric Abel (2008). *Introducing the PhonicStick: Preliminary evaluation with seven children.* Paper presented at the 13th Biennial Conference of the International Society for Augmentative and Alternative Communication Montreal, Canada.

Kevin Burton, Akashay Java, and Ian Soboroff (2009). *The ICWSM 2009 Spinn3r dataset.* Paper presented at the 3rd Annual Conference on Weblog and Social Media.

Rick Creech (2004). Rick Creech, 2004 Edwin and Esther Prentke AAC Distinguished Lecturer, from http://www.aacinstitute.org/Resources/PrentkeLecture/2004/RickCreech.html

Nestor Garay-Victoria and Julio Abascal (2005). Text prediction systems: a survey. *Universal Access in the Information Society, 4*, 188-203.

Alfred. C. Gimson and Alan Cruttenden (2001). *Gimson's Pronunciation of English*: Hodder Arnold.

Sharon L. Glennen and Denise C. DeCoste (1997). *The Handbook of Augmentative and Alternative Communication*: Thomson Delmar Learning.

Sheri Hunnicutt and Johan Caarlberger (2001). Improving Word prediction using markov models and heuristic methods. *Augmentative and Alternative Communication, 17*(4), 255-264.

David A. Koppenhaver and David E. Yoder, D (1992). Literacy issues in persons with severe speech and physical impairments. In R. Gaylord-Ross, Ed. (Ed.), *Issues and research in special education* (Vol. 2, pp. 156-201). NY: Teachers College Press, Columbia University, New York.

Cliff Kushler (1998). *AAC: Using a reduced keyboard.* Paper presented at the Technology and Persons with Disabilities Conference, Los Angeles, USA.

Gregory W. Lesher and Gerald J. Rinkus (2002). *Domain-specific word prediction for augmentatve communication.* Paper presented at the The RESNA '02 Annual Conference.

Gregory W. Lesher, Bryan J. Moulton, and Jeffrey D. Higginbotham (1998). Techniques for augmenting scanning communication. *Augmentative and Alternative Communication, 14*, 81-101.

Jianhua Li and Graeme Hirst (2005). *Semantic knowledge in word completion.* Paper presented at the 7th International ACM SIGACCESS Conference on Computers and Accessibility.

Nina Lindström and Irmeli Peronius (2010). *The PhonicStick nursery study: Can phonological awareness be initiated by using a speaking joystick.* Uppsala University.

Susan M. Lloyd (1998). *The Phonics Handbook.* Chigwell: Jolly Learning Ltd.

Robert C. Moore and William Lewis (2010). *Intelligent selection of language model training data.* Paper presented at the 48th Annual Meeting of the Association of Computational Linguistics.

James E. Schroeder (2005). *Improved spelling for persons with learning disabilities.* Paper presented at the The 20th Annual International Conference on Technology and Persons with Disabilities, California, USA.

Cyrus Shaoul and Chris Westbury (2009). A USENET corpus (2005-2009). University of Alberta, Canada.

Andrew L. Swiffin, John L. Arnott, and Alan Newell (1987). *The use of syntax in a predictive communication aid for the physically handicapped.* Paper presented at the RESNA 10th Annual Conference, San Jose, California.

Andrew L. Swiffin, John L. Arnott, Andrian J. Pickering, and Alan Newell (1987). Adaptive and predictive techniques in a communication prosthesis. *Augmentative and Alternative Communication, 3*(4), 181-191.

Keith Trnka, Debra Yarrington, Kathleen F. McCoy, and Christopher Pennington (2006). *Topic modeling in fringe word prediction for AAC.* Paper presented at the 11th International Conference on Intelligent User Interfaces.

Keith Trnka, John McCaw, Debra Yarrington, Kathleen F. McCoy, Christopher Pennington (2009). User interaction with word prediction: The effects of prediction quality. *ACM Transactions on Accessible Computing, 1*(3), 1-34.

Horabail S. Venkatagiri (1999). Efficient keyboard layouts for sequential access in augmentative and alternative communication. *Augmentative and Alternative Communication, 15*(2), 126-134.

Keith Vertanen and Per Ola Kristensson (2011). *The imagination of Crowds: Conversational AAC language modelling using crowdsourcing and large data sources.* Paper presented at the International Conference on Empirical Methods in Natural Language Processing (EMNLP), Edinburgh, United Kingdom.

Michael B. Williams (1995). *Transitions and transformations.* Paper presented at the 9th Annual Minspeak Conference, Wooster, OH.

Non-Syntactic Word Prediction for AAC

Karl Wiegand
Northeastern University
360 Huntington Ave
Boston, MA 02115, USA
wiegand@ccs.neu.edu

Rupal Patel, Ph.D.
Northeastern University
360 Huntington Ave
Boston, MA 02115, USA
r.patel@neu.edu

Abstract

Most icon-based augmentative and alternative communication (AAC) devices require users to formulate messages in syntactic order in order to produce syntactic utterances. Reliance on syntactic ordering, however, may not be appropriate for individuals with limited or emerging literacy skills. Some of these users may benefit from unordered message formulation accompanied by automatic message expansion to generate syntactically correct messages. Facilitating communication via unordered message formulation, however, requires new methods of prediction. This paper describes a novel approach to word prediction using semantic grams, or "sem-grams," which provide relational information about message components regardless of word order. Performance of four word-level prediction algorithms, two based on sem-grams and two based on n-grams, were compared on a corpus of informal blogs. Results showed that sem-grams yield accurate word prediction, but lack prediction coverage. Hybrid methods that combine n-gram and sem-gram approaches may be viable for unordered prediction in AAC.

1 Introduction

Many individuals with severe speech impairments rely on augmentative and alternative communication (AAC) devices to convey their thoughts and desires. Those with limited or emerging literacy skills may use icon-based systems, which often require that vocabulary items be selected in syntactic order to generate syntactically well-formed messages; however, selecting vocabulary items serially and in syntactic order can be physically and cognitively arduous depending on the icon organization scheme (Udwin and Yule, 1990). Moreover, AAC productions are often syntactically incomplete or incorrect (Van Balkom and Welle Donker-Gimbrere, 1996), perhaps for efficiency or due to limited linguistic abilities. For many users, unordered vocabulary selection may alleviate the physical and cognitive demands of message formulation and shift the onus of generating syntactically complete and accurate messages onto the AAC device. Although unordered message formulation schemes have been proposed (Karberis and Kouroupetroglou, 2002; Patel et al., 2004) and techniques have been developed for expanding incomplete input (McCoy et al., 1998), prediction has not been incorporated. This paper presents an initial step toward text prediction from a set of unordered vocabulary selections.

Rate enhancement is a commonly cited issue in AAC because aided message formulation rates are an order of magnitude slower than spoken interaction (Beukelman and Mirenda, 1998). Prediction is a common rate enhancement technique. Text prediction for AAC has primarily focused on well-ordered, syntactic input and has leveraged both semantic characteristics (Demasco and McCoy, 1992; Li and Hirst, 2005; Nikolova et al., 2010) and variations of n-grams (Lesher et al., 1998; Trnka et al., 2006). For example, semantic networks and linguistic rules have been used to predict missing function words and to apply affixes to content words (McCoy et al., 1998). The use of n-grams to predict text entry has been extensively studied at both the level of letters (Broerse and Zwaan, 1966; Suen, 1979; How and Kan, 2005) and words (Bickel et al., 2005). For example, memory based language models have been used to predict missing content words using trigrams (Van Den Bosch, 2006). Although some recent work has attempted to loosen syntactic requirements by including either left or right context, some directional context has historically been required (Van Den Bosch and Berck, 2009). Furthermore, word prediction approaches in AAC have typically been implemented for letter-by-letter message formulation (Koester and Levine, 1996; Koester and Levine, 1997; Lesher and Rinkus, 2002; Higginbotham et al., 2009). The current work is fundamentally novel in that: (1) no syntactic order is implied or required during either training or testing; and (2) the prediction is implemented at word level to accommodate icon-based interaction.

Previous work in information retrieval has explored relationships between words with regard to distance (Lin and Hovy, 2003; Lv and Zhai, 2009), grammatical purpose (Tzoukermann et al., 1997; Allan and Raghavan, 2002), and semantic characteristics (Westerman and Cribbin, 2000; Fang and Zhai, 2006; Hemayati et al., 2007), particularly for retrieving highly relevant documents or passages. One study in this area resulted in an approach called s-grams, a generalization of n-grams, in which the distance between words directly affects the strength of their semantic relationship (Järvelin et al., 2007). Another approach to predicting semantically related words is to use collocation to indicate topic changes within a moving window of fixed length (Matiasek and Baroni, 2003). Rather than relying on distance to indicate relationship strength, the current work combines frequency analysis with syntactic indications of semantic coherence.

1.1 Semantic Grams

Semantic grams, or "sem-grams," provide an alternative approach to quantifying the relationship between co-occurring words. A sem-gram is defined as a multiset of words that can appear together in a sentence (Table 1). In English, a sentence is one of the smallest units of language that is typically both coherent, in terms of semantic content, and cohesive, in that the semantic content is inter-related. Additionally, because sentences are demarcated with syntactic cues such as punctuation, semantically related items can be efficiently identified using sentence boundary detection (Kiss and Strunk, 2006). Thus, sem-grams leverage sentence-level co-occurrence to extract semantic content at different levels of granularity, depending on the allowable lengths of multisets. Sem-grams can be viewed as non-directional s-grams with a uniform weight applied to all relationships between any words in a given sentence.

Table 1: Example of Sem-Grams of Length 2

Sentence: "I like to play chess with my brother." **Filtered Words:** i, like, play, chess, brother	
Sem-grams and Counts:	
brother, chess (1)	brother, i (1)
brother, like (1)	brother, play (1)
chess, i (1)	chess, like (1)
chess, play (1)	i, like (1)
i, play (1)	like, play (1)

In a sentence of length L (in words), the number of n-grams of length n (in words), where $L \geq n$, is given by the expression $L - n + 3$, which includes the beginning and ending n-grams that contain null elements. By contrast, the number of sem-grams of length n is given by the expression $\binom{L}{n}$. Thus, there will typically be many more sem-grams of length n in a single sentence than n-grams of the same length. Unlike n-grams, it is not necessary for sem-grams to contain null elements because a sem-gram of length S with a null element is equivalent to a sem-gram of length $S - 1$ without null elements. Sem-grams of length one, containing a single word, are equivalent to the prior probability of that word.

1.2 Prediction Algorithms

Unordered word prediction poses the following problem: given a multiset of existing words E that have already been selected by a user and a set of candidate words C that the user may select from, which candidate word $c \in C$ is the user most likely to select in order to complete the message? As an initial step toward addressing this problem, the following four algorithms, two based on sem-grams and two based on n-grams, were compared:

S1: Naive Bayesian Sem-grams Given existing words E, rank all candidate words $c \in C$ in descending order of probability according to:

$$P(c|E) = P(c) \prod_{w \in E} P(w|c)$$

S1 is a modification of the Bayesian ranking of sem-grams in that it assumes independence of existing words to each other, conditional on the given candidate word. Using true Bayesian probabilities for sem-grams, the probability of a candidate word could be represented as the following for each $P(c|E)$, given $w \in E$ and $|E| = 3$:

$$\frac{P(c)P(w_1|c, w_2, w_3)P(w_2|c, w_3)P(w_3|c)}{P(w_1, w_2, w_3)}$$

The exact form of this equation depends on the ordering branch chosen, but it also requires joint probabilities for sem-grams of different lengths. Assuming conditional independence of the existing words to each other, S1 only requires sem-grams of length two.

S2: Independent Sem-grams Given existing words E, rank all candidate words $c \in C$ in descending order of probability according to:

$$P(c|E) = \prod_{w \in E} P(w, c)$$

The approach of S2 is a "hand of cards" approach that treats the message formulation task as a random drawing of sem-grams from a pool. While the formula above is specified for sem-grams of length 2, it can be extended to support sem-grams of any length.

N1: Naive Bayesian N-grams Given existing words E, rank all candidate words $c \in C$ in descending order of probability according to:

$$P(c|E) = P(c) \prod_{w \in E} P(w|c)$$

N1 is a copy of S1, except that the definition of the joint probability $P(w, c)$ includes the counts for n-grams that contain both w and c, regardless of order. This algorithm was designed to compare whether the information provided by n-grams can be used to approximate the information provided by sem-grams. N1 assigns high ranks to candidate words that are likely to appear adjacent to all other words in the sentence.

N2: Applied N-grams Given existing words E, rank all candidate words $c \in C$ in descending order of probability according to:

$$P(c|E) = \sum_{w \in E} P(w, c)$$

N2 is designed to leverage the strength of n-grams and rank candidate words based on the probability of them appearing adjacent to any of the existing words. N2 uses the same definition of joint probability as N1, where $P(w, c)$ includes the counts for n-grams that contain both w and c, irrespective of order.

2 Method

2.1 Corpus Selection and Preparation

Given the lack of large corpora of AAC message formulations (Lesher and Sanelli, 2000), approximations have often been used (Wandmacher and Antoine, 2006; Trnka and McCoy, 2007). Despite recent efforts to create AAC-like corpora (Vertanen and Kristensson, 2011), statistical prediction is often more effective with larger data sets. The Blog Authorship Corpus (Schler et al., 2006) was selected because it is freely available and tends to be written in an informal style, such as might be seen in diary entries or personal emails. The corpus is both large and diverse, comprising over 140 million words written by 19,320 bloggers in August 2004. The bloggers ranged in age from 13 - 48 and were equally divided between males and females.

To prepare the corpus, all blog posts were extracted as ASCII text. Every blog post was split into sentences using the PunktSentenceTokenizer (Kiss and Strunk, 2006) of the Natural Language Toolkit (NLTK) (Bird et al., 2009) and then split into words using the following regular expression:

```
\w+(\w*([\-\'\.]\w+)*)*
```

English stop words were removed according to a popular list (Ranks, 2012) and remaining words were stemmed using the NLTK's PorterStemmer, which is a modified implementation of the original Porter stemming algorithm (Porter, 1997). Finally, all stemmed words were examined for membership in a stemmed American-English dictionary (Ward,

Table 2: Sample Test Results for N1 and S1

Original Sentence: "but i went to church yesterday with the fam." **Target Stem:** went **Input Stems:** yesterday, church **N1 Candidate List:** went, morn, today, go, attend, work, afternoon, church, got, day, back, ... **S1 Candidate List:** went, go, church, today, got, day, like, time, just, well, one, get, peopl, ...
Original Sentence: "You never see signs like that in cities." **Target Stem:** like **Input Stems:** never, see, sign, citi **N1 Candidate List:** just, show, sign, realli, say, want, go, seen, thought, hall, citi, live, ... **S1 Candidate List:** never, will, like, can, go, love, one, just, know, want, get, live, time, ...
Original Sentence: "This semester Im taking six classes." **Target Stem:** class **Input Stems:** take, semest, six **N1 Candidate List:** next, month, class, hour, last, second, week, year, first, five, flag, ... **S1 Candidate List:** class, month, year, last, time, one, go, day, get, school, will, first, ...
Original Sentence: "Hey, they're in first, by a game and a half over the Yankees." **Target Stem:** game **Input Stems:** yanke, hey, first, half **N1 Candidate List:** game, stadium, like, hour, time, year, day, guy, hey, fan, say, one, two, ... **S1 Candidate List:** game, got, like, red, time, play, team, sox, hour, go, fan, one, get, day, ...

Note: Uncommon spelling (e.g. semest) is due to stemming.

2002). Any stemmed words not found in the dictionary were removed to further constrain the vocabulary and account for spelling errors and nonsensical text.

The corpus was then randomly split into a training and testing set based on authorship, with 80% of the authors (15,451) being placed in the training set and 20% of the authors (3,871) being placed in the testing set. The training set comprised over 7 million sentences written by 7,682 males and 7,768 females with a combined average age of 22 years. All n-gram and sem-gram statistics, with plus-one smoothing, were gathered using only sentences in the training set and both n-grams and sem-grams were limited to a word length of 2 (bigrams).

2.2 Evaluation

Testing was conducted on 2,000 sentences that were randomly selected from the test corpus. The same processing steps used during training were performed on the test sentences: stop words were removed, the remaining words were stemmed, and all stems not in the dictionary were filtered out. To avoid run-on sentences and sentence boundary detection errors, all test sentences were also truncated to a maximum of 20 words. The words in each test sentence were then shuffled and one word was removed at random and designated as the target word. Each of the four algorithms were provided the shuffled words as input; as output, each algorithm attempted to identify the target word by generating a ranked list of candidates (Table 2).

In addition to the shuffled multiset of input words, each algorithm required a seed list of candidate words. Ideally, all known words in the corpus would be used as candidate words. To constrain the computational requirements, the two algorithms based on n-grams (N1 and N2) were provided with the list of most frequently co-occurring words that appeared as n-grams with any of the multiset of input words, limited to the top 10 n-grams for a given input word. Similarly, each sem-gram algorithm (S1 and S2) received a list of most frequently co-occurring words that appeared as sem-grams with any of the multiset of input words, limited to the top 10 sem-grams for a given input word. With a limit of 19 input words (20 minus the target word), each algorithm received at most 190 unique candidate words to rank.

Two evaluation metrics were used to quantify the performance of each algorithm: (1) a boolean value that was true if the output list contained the target word in any position, indicating that the target word had been successfully predicted; (2) if the algorithm successfully predicted the target word, the algorithm received a positive integer score corresponding to the position of the target word in the output list, with lower scores indicating more accurate prediction. For example, if an algorithm suggested the target word as the first item in its ranked list, it received a score of 1; if it suggested the target word as the second item in its ranked list, it received a score of 2. For computational convenience, the output lists of each algorithm were truncated to the first 100 items; thus, if an algorithm's output list contained the target word in a position after 100, it was marked as failing to predict the target word.

3 Results

The n-gram algorithms successfully predicted 32% of the 2,000 test sentences while the sem-gram algorithms successfully predicted 22% (Table 3). Although both n-gram algorithms performed similarly, N1 consistently predicted the target word more accurately than N2. On average, N1 suggested the target word as the 16th word in its ranked list, where N2 suggested the target word as the 20th word in its list. While the sem-gram algorithms predicted fewer sentences than the n-gram algorithms, they were almost twice as accurate on sentences that they did predict. On average, S1 suggested the target word as the 9th word in its ranked list; for S2, the target word was the 13th item.

To further compare the effectiveness of sem-grams and n-grams, sentences were grouped according to their input length, from 1 to 19 words, and statistics were gathered for each algorithm on each sentence length (Table 4). For test sentences in which the algorithms were only given a single input word, both n-gram algorithms ranked the target word at least one full ranking higher than either sem-gram algorithm, thus giving more accurate predictions. For all other sentence lengths, the sem-gram algorithms were more accurate. Between the n-gram algorithms, N1 consistently predicted the target word more accurately and more often than N2. Similarly, S1 consistently predicted the target word more accurately and more often than S2.

Table 3: Summary of Results

	N1	**N2**	**S1**	**S2**
Sentences	2000	2000	2000	2000
# Predicted	647	649	435	435
% Predicted	32%	32%	22%	22%
Avg Score	16.26	19.70	9.04	12.67

For every input sentence length greater than one, S1 outperformed N1 in all gathered metrics. When comparing the prediction accuracy of N1 and S1, S1's prediction accuracy was also more stable, with N1's prediction accuracy continuing to degrade as the length of the input sentence increased (Figure 1).

4 Discussion

Message formulation using AAC devices has historically relied on serial selection of letters or words (icons). To produce syntactically correct messages for icon-based AAC, selection is often required to proceed in syntactic order. The current work aimed to facilitate unordered vocabulary selection through the use of text prediction. Results indicate that word prediction for unordered message formulation is viable using statistical approaches. Although the n-gram algorithms predicted a larger number of test sentences than the sem-gram algorithms, evaluation of the ranked output indicated that the sem-gram approaches were more accurate. Because n-grams assume that adjacent words are strongly related, it was expected that n-grams would provide more accurate prediction for shorter sentences; however, this advantage was not maintained as sentence length increased beyond two words. Prediction accuracy is likely to be more important in AAC devices because the cognitive demands of choosing from prediction lists can sometimes outweigh rate enhancements (Koester and Levine, 1996; Koester and Levine, 1997).

The use of bigrams may have resulted in poor accuracy of the n-gram algorithms because there were many more sem-grams than n-grams of length 2. Increasing n-gram length, up to a cardinality equal to the number of sem-grams of length 2, could allow n-

Table 4: Prediction Coverage (%) and Average Scores by Sentence Length

# Words	N1 %	N1 Avg	S1 %	S1 Avg	N2 %	N2 Avg	S2 %	S2 Avg
1	20.88%	3.44	12.05%	4.47	20.88%	3.42	12.05%	4.47
2	26.55%	6.07	19.47%	5.89	26.55%	6.32	19.47%	6.23
3	22.22%	7.64	16.89%	6.87	22.22%	9.82	16.89%	9.84
4	32.11%	10.46	22.94%	7.62	32.11%	11.91	22.94%	9.94
5	31.25%	12.13	21.88%	6.14	31.25%	14.02	21.88%	9.14
6	38.18%	15.25	26.67%	8.75	38.18%	17.68	26.67%	12.11
7	42.86%	16.17	29.46%	9.52	42.86%	21.77	29.46%	12.73
8	39.60%	18.08	25.74%	11.15	39.60%	22.00	25.74%	15.73
9	29.11%	19.13	20.25%	11.31	29.11%	23.48	20.25%	17.88
10	44.74%	24.47	35.53%	10.52	44.74%	23.56	35.53%	16.22
11	38.46%	28.55	26.92%	15.21	38.46%	26.80	26.92%	17.93
12	46.00%	23.39	14.00%	13.71	46.00%	41.26	14.00%	9.14
13	38.46%	24.47	25.64%	14.30	38.46%	34.07	25.64%	15.90
14	29.41%	26.30	14.71%	10.80	29.41%	39.10	14.71%	26.20
15	46.67%	32.14	20.00%	16.17	46.67%	36.79	20.00%	15.17
16	47.62%	25.70	28.57%	12.83	47.62%	30.50	28.57%	12.67
17	53.85%	23.14	38.46%	12.20	53.85%	35.14	38.46%	21.40
18	40.95%	38.35	25.71%	13.56	42.86%	43.07	25.71%	25.11
19	38.46%	23.80	38.46%	11.00	38.46%	52.40	38.46%	32.00

gram algorithms to potentially match or surpass the prediction accuracy of sem-grams. For unordered word prediction, this larger set of n-grams would need to be indexed in an order-independent manner, which would further increase computational demands. Such prediction lags, however, are unlikely to be tolerated by users as they engage in interactive tasks (Higginbotham et al., 2009).

Of the two n-gram algorithms, N1 outperformed N2 on both prediction coverage and accuracy. It was hypothesized, however, that N2 would yield more accurate predictions because the target word was defined to be adjacent to at least one of the input words. It was expected that N1 would unfairly reward candidate words that had appeared adjacent to each input word in the training set, while punishing more desirable candidate words that had not appeared adjacent to some of the input words. Perhaps this bias was not evident in the current corpus because plus-one smoothing removed all zero probabilities for adjacency likelihoods. Additionally, N1 may have been more successful because it favored candidates that were related to all input words rather than candidates that were strongly related to just a subset of the input words.

Despite the encouraging prediction coverage of n-grams and the prediction accuracy of sem-grams, approximately two-thirds of the test sentences were not predicted by any of the algorithms. One possible explanation may relate to the decision to seed each algorithm with only the top 10 most frequent words that co-occurred with each input word. Ideally, each algorithm would have considered all words in the vocabulary as candidate words; however, because there were almost 40,000 unique stems in the processed corpus, the computational requirements were prohibitive for this initial implementation. An open empirical question is whether increasing the seed values to include a larger set of co-occurring words would result in greater prediction coverage. It should be noted, however, that while seeding sem-grams with more candidate words may improve prediction coverage, it is unlikely to increase prediction accuracy for the n-gram approaches.

Icon-based AAC devices typically have active vocabularies with much fewer than 40,000 words, which may negate the need for seeding candidate words. For example, two commonly used icon

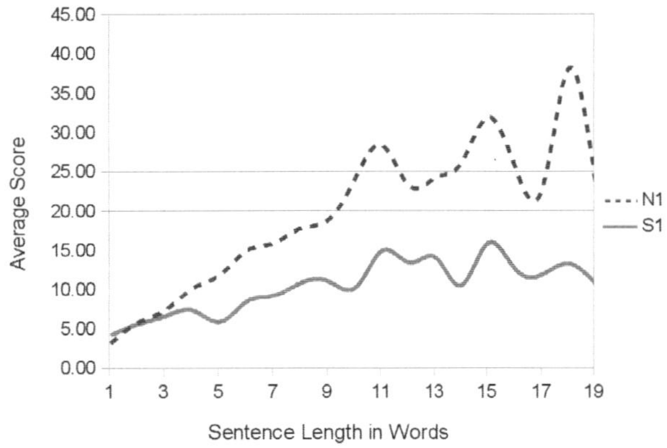

Figure 1: Average score per sentence length for both N1 and S1 (lower scores indicate more accurate prediction).

sets, the Widgit Symbol Set and the Mayer-Johnson Picture Communication Symbol collection, each contain approximately 11,000 icons (Widgit, 2012; Mayer-Johnson, 2012). While a large dictionary was used in this work to provide a conservative estimate of prediction performance, it is possible that using a smaller and more representative AAC vocabulary would improve prediction coverage and accuracy. Additionally, restricting vocabulary size would also reduce computational demands, making it more feasible to use all vocabulary words as candidates.

5 Conclusion and Future Directions

The current work provides a promising approach to word prediction for AAC users who may benefit from unordered message formulation. Sem-grams make use of co-occurrence between words within a sentence to improve prediction accuracy. While n-grams have historically provided a strong foundation for word prediction in letter-by-letter systems, results indicate that they can also be used for unordered word prediction, although they are not as accurate as sem-grams. A hybrid approach that seeds both types of algorithms with a superset of candidate words and merges the prediction lists may simultaneously exhibit the wide prediction coverage of n-grams and the high prediction accuracy of sem-grams. Such a hybrid approach could enhance the speed of unordered message formulation and increase social engagement.

Additional improvements to this work may be possible using the breadth of information available within well-documented and comprehensive corpora. For example, while the Blog Authorship Corpus included age and gender information about each blogger, this information was not used in the present study. To tailor prediction to individual users, it may be possible to limit the available vocabulary and gram-based statistics to information gathered from users of similar age and gender. This may improve prediction accuracy for both n-gram and sem-gram algorithms, as well as provide an approach to designing icon-based AAC devices that can evolve and adapt to users as their needs and abilities mature, potentially even suggesting new vocabulary words as the users age.

Acknowledgments

The authors would like to thank the creators of the Blog Authorship Corpus for making the corpus freely available for non-commercial research purposes. The material in this paper is based upon work supported by the National Science Foundation under Grant No. 0914808. Any opinions, findings, conclusions, or recommendations expressed in this material are those of the authors and do not necessarily reflect the views of the National Science Foundation.

References

J. Allan and H. Raghavan. 2002. Using part-of-speech patterns to reduce query ambiguity. In *Proceedings of the 25th annual international ACM SIGIR conference on Research and development in information retrieval*, SIGIR '02, pages 307–314, New York, NY, USA. ACM.

D. Beukelman and P. Mirenda. 1998. *Augmentation and alternative communication: Management of severe communication disorders in children and adults.* Paul H. Brookes, Baltimore.

S. Bickel, P. Haider, and T. Scheffer. 2005. Predicting sentences using n-gram language models. In *Proceedings of the conference on Human Language Technology and Empirical Methods in Natural Language Processing*, HLT '05, pages 193–200, Stroudsburg, PA, USA. Association for Computational Linguistics.

S. Bird, E. Klein, and E. Loper. 2009. *Natural Language Processing with Python.* O'Reilly Media, 1 edition, July.

A. C. Broerse and E. J. Zwaan. 1966. The information value of initial letters in the identification of words. *Journal of Verbal Learning and Verbal Behavior*, 5(5):441–446, October.

P. Demasco and K. McCoy. 1992. Generating text from compressed input: an intelligent interface for people with severe motor impairments. *Commun. ACM*, 35(5):68–78, May.

H. Fang and C. Zhai. 2006. Semantic term matching in axiomatic approaches to information retrieval. In *Proceedings of the 29th annual international ACM SIGIR conference on Research and development in information retrieval*, SIGIR '06, pages 115–122, New York, NY, USA. ACM.

R. Hemayati, W. Meng, and C. Yu. 2007. Semantic-based grouping of search engine results using WordNet. In *Proceedings of the joint 9th Asia-Pacific web and 8th international conference on web-age information management conference on Advances in data and web management*, APWeb/WAIM'07, pages 678–686, Berlin, Heidelberg. Springer-Verlag.

J. Higginbotham, A. Bisantz, M. Sunm, K. Adams, and F. Yik. 2009. The effect of context priming and task type on augmentative communication performance. *Augmentative and Alternative Communication*, 25(1):19–31.

Y. How and M. Kan. 2005. Optimizing predictive text entry for short message service on mobile phones. In *Human Computer Interfaces International (HCII 05)*.

A. Järvelin, A. Järvelin, and K. Järvelin. 2007. s-grams: Defining generalized n-grams for information retrieval. *Information Processing & Management*, 43(4):1005–1019, July.

G. Karberis and G. Kouroupetroglou. 2002. Transforming spontaneous telegraphic language to Well-Formed greek sentences for alternative and augmentative communication. In *Proceedings of the Second Hellenic Conference on AI: Methods and Applications of Artificial Intelligence*, SETN '02, pages 155–166, London, UK, UK. Springer-Verlag.

T. Kiss and J. Strunk. 2006. Unsupervised multilingual sentence boundary detection. *Comput. Linguist.*, 32(4):485–525, December.

H. Koester and S. Levine. 1996. Effect of a word prediction feature on user performance. *Augmentative and Alternative Communication*, 12(3):155–168.

H. Koester and S. Levine. 1997. Keystroke-level models for user performance with word prediction. *Augmentative and Alternative Communication*, 13(4).

G. Lesher and G. Rinkus. 2002. Domain-Specific word prediction for augmentative communication. In *Proceedings of the RESNA 2002 Annual Conference*.

G. Lesher and C. Sanelli. 2000. A Web-Based system for autonomous text corpus generation. In *Proceedings of ISAAC*.

G. Lesher, B. Moulton, and J. Higginbotham. 1998. Techniques for augmenting scanning communication. *Augmentative and Alternative Communication*, 14(2):81–101, January.

J. Li and G. Hirst. 2005. Semantic knowledge in word completion. In *Proceedings of the 7th international ACM SIGACCESS conference on Computers and accessibility*, Assets '05, pages 121–128, New York, NY, USA. ACM.

C. Lin and E. Hovy. 2003. Automatic evaluation of summaries using n-gram co-occurrence statistics. In *Proceedings of the 2003 Conference of the North American Chapter of the Association for Computational Linguistics on Human Language Technology - Volume 1*, NAACL '03, pages 71–78, Stroudsburg, PA, USA. Association for Computational Linguistics.

Y. Lv and C. Zhai. 2009. Positional language models for information retrieval. In *Proceedings of the 32nd international ACM SIGIR conference on Research and development in information retrieval*, SIGIR '09, pages 299–306, New York, NY, USA. ACM.

J. Matiasek and M. Baroni. 2003. Exploiting long distance collocational relations in predictive typing. In *Proceedings of the 2003 EACL Workshop on Language Modeling for Text Entry Methods*, TextEntry '03, pages 1–8, Stroudsburg, PA, USA. Association for Computational Linguistics.

Mayer-Johnson. 2012. Picture communication symbols collections (http://www.mayer-johnson.com). March.

K. McCoy, C. Pennington, and A. Badman. 1998. Compansion: From research prototype to practical integration. *Natural Language Engineering*, 4(01):73–95.

S. Nikolova, M. Tremaine, and P. Cook. 2010. Click on bake to get cookies: guiding word-finding with semantic associations. In *Proceedings of the 12th international ACM SIGACCESS conference on Computers and accessibility*, ASSETS '10, pages 155–162, New York, NY, USA. ACM.

R. Patel, S. Pilato, and D. Roy. 2004. Beyond linear syntax: An Image-Oriented communication aid. *Journal of Assistive Technology Outcomes and Benefits*, (1):57–66.

M. F. Porter. 1997. Readings in information retrieval. chapter An algorithm for suffix stripping, pages 313–316. Morgan Kaufmann Publishers Inc., San Francisco, CA, USA.

Ranks. 2012. English stopwords (http://www.ranks.nl), March.

J. Schler, M. Koppel, S. Argamon, and J. Pennebaker. 2006. Effects of age and gender on blogging. In *Proceedings of 2006 AAAI Spring Symposium on Computational Approaches for Analyzing Weblogs*.

C. Suen. 1979. n-Gram statistics for natural language understanding and text processing. *Pattern Analysis and Machine Intelligence, IEEE Transactions on*, PAMI-1(2):164–172, April.

K. Trnka and K. McCoy. 2007. Corpus studies in word prediction. In *Proceedings of the 9th international ACM SIGACCESS conference on Computers and accessibility*, Assets '07, pages 195–202, New York, NY, USA. ACM.

K. Trnka, D. Yarrington, K. McCoy, and C. Pennington. 2006. Topic modeling in fringe word prediction for AAC. In *Proceedings of the 11th international conference on Intelligent user interfaces*, IUI '06, pages 276–278, New York, NY, USA. ACM.

E. Tzoukermann, J. Klavans, and C. Jacquemin. 1997. Effective use of natural language processing techniques for automatic conflation of multi-word terms: the role of derivational morphology, part of speech tagging, and shallow parsing. *SIGIR Forum*, 31(SI):148–155, July.

O. Udwin and W. Yule. 1990. Augmentative communication systems taught to cerebral palsied children - a longitudinal study:I. the acquisition of signs and symbols, and syntactic aspects of their use over time. *British Journal of Disorders of Communication*, 25(3):295–309, January.

H. Van Balkom and M. Welle Donker-Gimbrere. 1996. A psycholinguistic approach to graphic language use. *Augmentative and alternative communication: European Perspectives*, pages 153–170.

A. Van Den Bosch and P. Berck. 2009. Memory-based machine translation and language modeling. In *The Prague Bulletin of Mathematical Linguistics.*

A. Van Den Bosch. 2006. Scalable classification-based word prediction and confusible correction. *Traitement Automatique des Langues*, 46(2):39–63.

K. Vertanen and P. O. Kristensson. 2011. The imagination of crowds: Conversational AAC language modeling using crowdsourcing and large data sources. In *Proceedings of the Conference on Empirical Methods in Natural Language Processing (EMNLP)*, pages 700–711. ACL.

T. Wandmacher and J. Antoine. 2006. Training language models without appropriate language resources: Experiments with an AAC system for disabled people. In *Proceedings of LREC.*

G. Ward. 2002. Moby word list: American english (http://www.gutenberg.org/ebooks/3201). Public domain in the USA.

S. J. Westerman and T. Cribbin. 2000. Mapping semantic information in virtual space: dimensions, variance and individual differences. *International Journal of Human-Computer Studies*, 53(5):765–787, November.

Widgit. 2012. About symbols (http://www.widgit.com), March.

Assisting Social Conversation between Persons with Alzheimer's Disease and their Conversational Partners

Nancy L. Green
UNC Greensboro
Dept. of Computer Science
Greensboro, NC, USA
nlgreen@uncg.edu

Curry Guinn
UNC Wilmington
Dept. of Computer Science
Wilmington, NC, USA
guinnc@uncw.edu

Ronnie W. Smith
East Carolina University
Dept. of Computer Science
Greenville, NC, USA
rws@cs.ecu.edu

Abstract

The number of people with dementia of the Alzheimer's type (DAT) continues to grow. One of the significant impacts of this disease is a decline in the ability to communicate using natural language. This decline in language facility often results in decreased social interaction and life satisfaction for persons with DAT and their caregivers. One possible strategy to lessen the effects of this loss of language facility is for the unaffected conversational partner (Facilitator) to "co-construct" short autobiographical stories from the life of the DAT-affected conversational partner (Storyteller). It has been observed that a skilled conversational partner can facilitate co-constructed narrative with individuals who have mild to moderate DAT. Developing a computational model of this type of co-constructed narrative would enable assistive technology to be developed that can monitor a conversation between a Storyteller and Facilitator. This technology could provide context-sensitive suggestions to an unskilled Facilitator to help maintain the flow of conversation. This paper describes a framework in which the necessary computational model of co-constructed narrative can be developed. An analysis of the fundamental elements of such a model will be presented.

1 Introduction

According to the Alzheimer's Association [2009], 13% of Americans over the age of 65 present with AD [Alzheimer's Disease]. The decline in language associated with AD can result in decreased social interaction and life satisfaction for persons with AD and their caregivers. In particular, persons with AD begin to feel a loss of their personal identity. "Reminiscent therapy is an example of an intervention activity that can reveal and support a person's identity. Even the family can participate and play a major role to support their relative" (Cohene et al. 2005).

It has been suggested that if caregivers can learn communication techniques to enhance social conversation with individuals affected by dementia of the Alzheimer's type (DAT), it may make a significant difference in the quality of life of the persons with DAT, as well as reduce stress on their caregivers (Dijkstra et al. 2004). One recommended technique (Moore and Davis 2002; Waller 2006) is for the unaffected conversational partner (called the Facilitator in this paper) to "co-construct" short autobiographical vignettes with the DAT-affected conversational partner (called the Storyteller in this paper). Typically, such "small stories" (Bamberg and Georgakopoulou 2008) present the teller's self-identity (e.g., hard-working, frugal, etc.). According to Cheepen (1988), co-constructed narrative is common in social conversation. Furthermore, skilled conversational partners can facilitate co-constructed narrative with individuals who have mild to moderate DAT (Davis 2005; Davis & Maclagan 2009; Davis 2010). A co-constructed narrative produced by a person with DAT in conversation with skilled Facilitators is illustrated in Figure 1. Increased social interaction can improve quality of life by enabling persons with DAT to remain socially engaged, which in turn may reduce their health problems as well as delay memory loss (Davis and Pope 2009; Lenchuk and Swain 2010).

/* orientation: */
1. GM: I just lived in a regular farm home. Farmed cotton, corn, eh-everything you…grow on a farm.
2. BD: That's right.
/* complicating action: */
3. GM: I had a big ol' cotton bag tied around me, pickin' a hundred pounds of cotton … UhhmmHmm.
4. BD: A hundred pounds? An' you so tiny!
5. GM: Huh?
6. LM: You're a tiny person to be carrying that much cotton.
7. GM: I decided one day I'd pick a hundred pounds. Guess how much!
8. LM: How much?
/* resolution: */
9. GM: A hundred and three.
10. LM: Oooohh.
11. BD: Wow.
12. GM: I went over.
13. BD: That's fantastic.
/* evaluation: */
14. GM: A hundred and three—you've got to grab it to…get a hundred and three pounds of cotton in one day.

Figure 1. An excerpt from Shenk et al. (2002, p. 409) of a conversation between GM, a person with early moderate DAT, and her skilled conversational partners BD and LM. We added annotations highlighting narrative elements (Labov 1972).

While there have been several notable efforts in the area of communication training for caregivers of persons with DAT (see section 2.1), none have focused on assistive technology for improving communication in real-time as the conversation is occurring. This paper presents a framework for developing a natural language processing system, ASSIST (Assistive Story Intervention Technology), which can listen to the conversation between a person with DAT and his conversational partner and provide context-sensitive suggestions to the unaffected participant to help maintain the flow of conversation. In particular, ASSIST will help the unaffected partner to co-construct the autobiographical stories of the participant with DAT. To build a system such as ASSIST will require development of a novel computational model of narrative co-construction and other communication-enhancing techniques for conversation with persons with DAT. After reviewing related research efforts, we present an analysis of the unique elements of the required computational model including an NLU component designed to interpret the sometimes disfluent utterances of a Storyteller with DAT, a Dialogue/Story Manager which recognizes the discourse goals of the Storyteller and plans dialogue acts that the Facilitator could use to co-construct the narrative, and an NLG/Coach that provides the Facilitator with suggestions on what to say next to co-construct the narrative and sustain the conversation.

2 Related Research

2.1 DAT Caregiver Communication

For the most part, communication training for caregivers of persons with DAT has used non-technological modes of active instruction such as role playing with human trainers (Ripich et al. 1998, Burgio et al. 2001) and individualized one-on-one coaching (McCallion et al. 1999, Bourgeois et al. 2004). Irvine et al. (2003) describe a computer program that enables a user to observe videos of conversations in which nurse aids demonstrate use of recommended communication techniques in conversation with patients. Davis and colleagues have developed a range of computer-based training materials (Davis and Smith 2009; Smith, Davis et al. 2010) providing information on stereotypes of aging and dementia, communication changes in dementia, and communication techniques such as "quilting" (Moore and Davis 2003), in which the caregiver repeats or paraphrases statements given by the person with DAT that seem to be elaborations or evaluations of elements of a narrative. Green and colleagues developed and evaluated a menu-based interactive system for training caregivers to engage more effectively in social conversation with persons with DAT (Green 2002; Green and Davis 2003; Green, Lawton and Davis 2004; Green 2005a; Green and Bevan 2009).

2.2 Augmentative and Alternative Communication Technology

There has been recent interest in developing reminiscence technology for the general population, e.g., (Cosley et al. 2009; Petrelli et al. 2009). Waller (2006) cites the need to develop augmentative and alternative communication systems for people with complex communication needs (CCN) to engage in conversational narrative. One assistive software package, Talk:About, enables someone with CCN to edit pre-stored text during a conversation, enabling the user to retell autobiographical stories. Phototalk (Allen et al. 2008) allows people with aphasia to manage personal photographs to support face-to-face communication. Non-technology-based reminiscence therapy has been used in dementia care (Hsieh 2003; Woods et al. 2005) and gerontological nursing (Burnside 1996).

CIRCA is a computer system that people with dementia and caregivers can use together to prompt reminiscing by providing multimedia stimuli (Alm et al. 2007). CIRCA provides touch-screen access to hypermedia presenting non-personalized reminiscence materials (e.g., photographs and music of a certain era). In a controlled study, CIRCA was compared to traditional reminiscence (TRAD) sessions with materials provided by caregivers (Astell et al. 2010). In TRAD sessions, "the caregivers worked very hard to keep the interaction going, particularly by asking lots of questions. These were typically closed questions … that did not encourage either initiation or choosing [topics] by people with dementia … caregivers offer more choice during CIRCA sessions and are much more likely to encourage the people with dementia to decide what they want to look at and talk about" (p. 7).

Baecker and colleagues (Cohene et al. 2005; Massimi et al. 2008; Smith et al. 2009; Damianakis et al. 2010) have been investigating creation and use of personalized DVD-based multimedia biographies by persons with AD and mild cognitive impairments. These researchers note that organizations such as the National Institutes of Health recommend creation of personal reminiscence aids such as photographs to help maintain the affected individual's sense of identity (Smith et al. 2009). "The loss of identity is among the most devastating effects of Alzheimer's disease … it is possible that sensitively designed technologies may help compensate for identity loss by acting as external memory or conversational aids" (Massimi et al. 2008). Roark et al. (2011) report on an initial study of technology-assisted co-construction. However, their emphasis is very different from ours and is focused on assisting with word and phrase completion of general conversation involving typewritten communication.

2.3 Narrative Technology

Cassell's research group has focused on systems that interact with human storytellers. In GrandChair, an embodied conversational agent (ECA) portrays a grandchild who elicits autobiographical stories from elderly users by providing feedback (through speech recognition technology) while the stories are recorded (Smith 2000). Story Listening Systems (SLS) use technology to encourage young children to create personally relevant stories in order to improve their oral linguistic skills (Cassell 2004). Sam the CastleMate (Ryokai, Vaucelle, & Cassell 2003) is an SLS in which SAM, an ECA, listens to the child's stories (also using speech recognition technology) and tells stories to the child. Natural language processing and statistical machine learning tools have been applied to the problem of automatic plot analysis of children's stories (Halpin et al. 2004; Passonneau et al. 2007) and to creation of story understanding tools (Elson and McKeown 2009).

Other researchers have focused on story generation. Narrative scholars distinguish the *fabula* – events in a fictional world – and *sujhet* – the author's choices in presentation of selected elements of the fabula. (Note that in our future ASSIST system, the fabula is already established when the user's stories are collected; the role of ASSIST is to facilitate the retelling, i.e., the sujhet.) Most past natural language generation research in narrative has focused on prose rather than dialogue (Callaway 2000; Theune et al. 2007; Hervás et al. 2006). Piwek and Stoyanchev (2010) have investigated automatically transforming human-authored narrative prose into dialogue performed by virtual characters as a way of presenting educational information.

3 Corpus Analysis

Most previous computationally-oriented research on human-human dialogue has focused on task-driven dialogue, i.e., dialogue intended to achieve an agent's (or agents' collaborative) task goals such as making a travel reservation. In contrast, ASSIST is modeling social conversation containing co-constructed narrative. That is, through certain conversational moves one participant (the Facilitator) can enable the other participant (the Storyteller) to retell short autobiographical stories, despite the Storyteller's language and memory problems associated with DAT. The model will be informed by interdisciplinary research on retained language competencies of speakers with DAT (Davis 2005; Guendouzi and Muller 2006), as well as by our own statistical and qualitative analyses of the Carolina Conversations Collection (CCC) Corpus (Davis and Pope 2009; Pope and Davis 2011). The CCC corpus includes 400 recorded and transcribed conversations between researchers and students and 125 persons with DAT. Our model will be constructed by annotating and analyzing a set of the DAT conversations as described in more detail in Section 4. The overall goal is to analyze the efficacy of narrative co-construction and other communication-enhancing techniques proposed in previous studies of language of persons with DAT (e.g., Ripich and Wykle, 1996; Ramanathan 1997; Moore and Davis 2002; Santo Pietro and Ostuni, 2003) and to possibly identify other effective techniques. As context for discussion of the necessary analysis of the CCC, we will first present a high-level description of the necessary system architecture.

4 System Architecture

The ASSIST architecture is shown in Figure 2. While a Storyteller and Facilitator converse, ASSIST listens with the goals of detecting potential problems in the flow of conversation and of providing suggestions to the Facilitator on what to say next to co-construct the narrative and sustain conversation. The tasks of the **NLU component** include syntactic and semantic interpretation and reference resolution; note that these tasks may require use of biographical information about the Storyteller to help interpret disfluencies characteristic of AD language. Another key task of NLU is to recognize the Facilitator's use of grounding acts, which play a key role in narrative co-construction and in sustaining conversation in general. One of the **Dialogue/Story Manager's** tasks is to recognize the conversational goals of the Storyteller's contributions, including narrative goals. Having recognized the Storyteller's current goal, the other task of the Dialogue Manager is to plan the next dialogue act that the Facilitator could use to continue to co-construct the Storyteller's narrative. The Dialogue Manager may use biographical information about the Storyteller in both tasks, i.e., to help recognize narrative goals and to select content when planning the next suggested narrative act. The **NLG/Coach component** is responsible for providing the Facilitator with one or more suggested utterances that the Facilitator could say next. Based upon the current discourse state, the suggested dialogue acts provided by the Dialogue/Story Manager, and a coaching model, the NLG/Coach component chooses one or more Facilitator acts and realizes them. In the remainder of this section we will describe the required analyses of the corpus needed to inform the development of the computational model for each of these main architectural components.

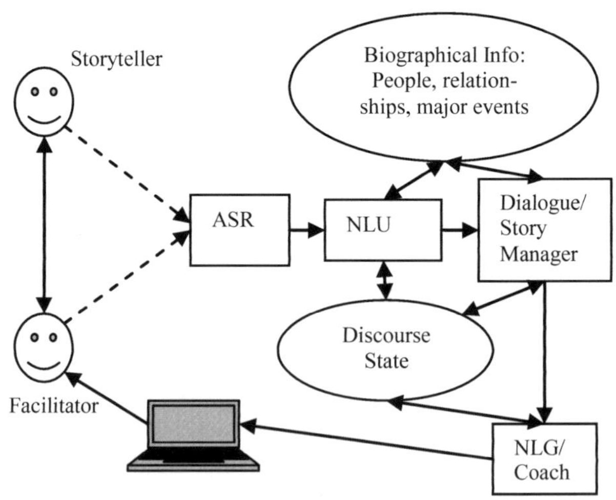

Figure 2. ASSIST system architecture.

4.1 Dialogue/Story Manager

Part of the CCC corpus study will analyze narrative features of the dialogue and related pragmatic and affective features. Coelho (1998) surveys various approaches to narrative analysis in discourse of communicatively impaired adults. Our analysis will reflect the following characteristics of conversational narrative identified in narrative studies (Georgakopoulou and Goutsos 1997; Polkinghorne 1996):

- Conversational narratives have a characteristic structure, consisting of an abstract, orientation, one or more complicating actions, resolution, evaluation, and coda (Labov 1972). Note that only the complicating action and resolution are required. We will annotate this structure, as shown in Figure 1.
- They often convey the teller's attitudes and feelings about narrated events, i.e., although not required the evaluation is often present. Furthermore, the objective truth of the events is not important. We will also annotate polarity and intensity of the evaluation (Wiebe et al. 2005).
- Conversational narrative is context-dependent, i.e., dependent upon the audience and the situation in which it is told. We will also annotate features of the social context such as the age, gender, and relationship of the conversational participants.
- There are culture-specific properties that make a story tellable. We will annotate the recurrent cultural themes in the corpus informed by previous studies of narrative themes as in, e.g., (Polanyi 1985; Shenk et al. 2002).

Although the above characteristics were derived from studies of narrative in other populations than in speakers with DAT, there is preliminary evidence of their applicability to ASSIST. For example, by examining retellings of the same stories over time, Davis and Maclagan (2009) found that "With AD story-tellers, components vanish from surface retellings, particularly the abstract/orientation. Instead, the listener is presented with parts of the story's complicating action or an evaluative comment that includes a fragment of the complication and its result"; yet, "even when full stories are not retrieved … the emotion is still conveyed to the listener" (p. 152). Comparing life-history narratives of two rural American older women, one with dementia and one without, Shenk et al. (2002, p. 410) found similar "major themes that are consistent with rural American cultural values", e.g., strong family ties, hard work, and religious faith.

Based on analysis of the stories in the CCC, we plan to define a set of abstract narrative schemas. A schema will include constraints on tellability with respect to audience characteristics (e.g., age, gender, social relationship) and current topic, and a specification of narrative goals (e.g. present the Storyteller as having been hard-working and thrifty). Each schema will be structured according to Labov's elements of a well-formed narrative. The schemas will be derived by analysis of the CCC corpus and informed by previous studies of narrative themes.

In addition to analysis of features suggested by previous narrative studies, we will analyze occurrences of pragmatic features that may be used by a speaker with DAT to compensate for difficulties when telling a story. For example, Davis and Maclagan (2009) studied both how use of unfilled pauses and pauses with fillers (e.g., "oh", "um", or a formulaic phrase) changed over time in DAT discourse, and also the placement of filled and unfilled pauses with respect to narrative components. Pauses in earlier stages of DAT correlated with word-finding problems, while pauses in later stages marked narrative components. Thus, Davis and Maclagan hypothesize that pauses in the later stages correlate with search for the next component of the story. Also, the Facilitator's contribution to the co-constructed narrative will be analyzed, e.g., when the Facilitator invites the Storyteller to begin a particular story and responds appropriately to an element supplied by the Storyteller. Development of the computational model for the Dialogue/StoryManager requires consideration of both the narrative structure and these related pragmatic and affective features.

4.2 Natural Language Understanding (NLU)

A skilled Facilitator tries to anticipate the kinds of problems that a Storyteller with DAT might have in a conversation and provide appropriate support so that the frequency and severity of DAT-related disfluencies will be reduced. In the event that a disfluency does occur, the Facilitator tries to provide support either by trying to resolve the particular kind of disfluency via a direct or indirect repair or by trying to advance the story without necessarily resolving the disfluency. Therefore, in order for ASSIST to facilitate conversation between a Storyteller and his or her conversational partner, the NLU module must be able to listen to a conversation and be able to determine the following: (1) How fluent was the Storyteller in the prior utterances? (2) If the Storyteller exhibited any issues with fluency, what was the nature of the problems? (3) What conversational strategies did the Facilitator use to help alleviate issues related to fluency, if any, before, during or after the Storyteller's utterances? Addressing these questions requires an analysis of the Carolina Conversations Collection (CCC) as discussed below.

Fluency

Considerable research has investigated the language of individuals with DAT (Bucks et al. 2000; Martin and Fedio 1983; Phillips et al. 1996; Sabat 1994). Linguistic features such as long pauses, restarts, repetitions, unfinished sentences, pronominal reference mistakes, and filler phrases are prevalent in the spontaneous speech of persons with DAT. Further, research has shown deviations from the norm in syntactic measurements such as part-of-speech rates (nouns, verbs, adjectives, pronouns), richness of vocabulary (Type Token Ratio, Brunet's Index, Honore's Statistic), and semantic cohesion in text (Singh and Bookless 1997). It is necessary to analyze the CCC corpus to determine the statistical prevalence of these phenomena within the corpus with a goal of making predictions about the relative fluency of an utterance based on the presence or dearth of these measurements.

Conversational Repair Strategies

Once we have a calculation for the level of fluency of each turn that a person with DAT (the Storyteller) takes in the dialog, we can then look at the surrounding behavior of the Facilitator. One of our hypotheses is that there are certain strategies that will be beneficial in increasing the fluency of DAT utterances. For example, narrative co-construction techniques recommended for caregivers of persons with DAT (Moore and Davis 2002) will be annotated in the corpus, including two-syllable go-ahead phrases (e.g., "uh huh", "really", "ok"), paraphrases and repetitions, and indirect questions. Most of these strategies can be described as

1. BD: You were telling me about your husband.
2. Did he preach sermons?
3. GM: My husband?
4. BD: Would he be a preacher?
5. GM: Yes. He was a preacher that preached "hell hot and heaven beautiful!"
(*They both laugh.*)
6. BD: Heaven beautiful …
7. GM: Yes. "Hell hot and heaven beautiful!" That was one of his messages. I don't know… he preached all right. He was an Evangelistic-type preacher.
8. BD: I bet you went many places!
9. GM: Well, I had my family while I was young and couldn't go. I mean … you can't go with a bunch of little kids.
10. BD: No you can't.

Figure 3. An excerpt from Davis (2005, p. 141) of a conversation between GM, a person with early moderate DAT, and her skilled conversational partner BD.

grounding acts (Clark and Schaefer 1989). The following seven types of grounding acts occur in co-constructed narratives:

- **Continued attention**. These utterances, such as "That's right" (line 2 in Figure 1), indicate that the listener is paying attention to the speaker.
- **Relevant next contribution**. By these utterances, which we call *forward grounding* moves, the conversational participant continues the conversation with a question or comment that requires that he or she understood the previous speaker's utterance (e.g. lines 2, 4, and 8 in Figure 3).
- **Acknowledgement**. In addition to showing continued attention, these utterances provide an assessment, e.g. "wow" (line 11 in Figure 1).
- **Demonstration**. The conversational participant paraphrases a previous utterance of his own or of the other participants (e.g. line 4 of Fig. 3).
- **Display**. The listener repeats all or part of the previous utterance verbatim (e.g. line 6 in Figure 3).

- **Completion**. The conversational participant completes the utterance of the previous speaker.
- **Request for repair**. The listener indicates that he or she did not understand all or part of the previous utterance (e.g. line 3 in Figure 3).

The first five types are described in Clark and Schaefer (1989) while *Completion* and *Request for Repair* have been described in Traum (1994) and elsewhere. Of particular importance is the use of the *Relevant next contribution* or forward grounding move. Persons with DAT have difficulty with lexical retrieval and other memory tasks associated with generating language (Martin and Fedio 1983). An effective Facilitator will provide lexical priming and syntactic structures to help these memory tasks (Ramanathan 1997; Orange 2001).

Unlike previous research on techniques for automatic grading of children's written stories (e.g. Halpin et al. 2004), the contributions of the partner with DAT will not necessarily be counted as disfluent when details are missing, incorrect, or presented out of temporal sequence. As discussed previously, in conversation with people with DAT narrative elements are often missing and a narrative may consist of as little as a fragment of the complicating action and the evaluation. The Facilitator's role is not to correct inaccuracies, to demand clarification, or to tell the story for the Storyteller. For example, suppose the Storyteller said, "I uh used to have a farm there." Suppose that the word "there" is not something that the Facilitator can resolve based on the context of the conversation. So, from the Facilitator's point of view, to understand the story better, it might make sense to resolve the word "there" by asking, "Where was your farm?" However, a more appropriate response would be a grounding move that prompts the continuation of the story without asking a wh-question: "Really? You were a farmer?"

By analyzing the CCC corpus, we can determine the prevalence of the above grounding actions by the Facilitator. Based on the fluency of the Storyteller's subsequent utterances, we can determine the relative effectiveness of these strategies on increasing or decreasing Storyteller fluency. This analysis can be further refined by examining the types of disfluency exhibited by the Storyteller before and after these grounding actions. In turn, this data can be used to make predictions about what repair strategies a conversational participant might use in response to a particular type of disfluent utterance. Based on the analysis techniques presented in Cherney et. al. (1998), we will be able to examine the extent to which greater fluency in the Storyteller utterances leads to more complete and coherent narrative. This anaylsis is also used in the development of the NLG/Coach module as described below.

4.3 NLG/Coach

Based upon the current discourse state and the suggested dialogue acts provided by the Dialogue/Story Manager, the NLG/Coach component must choose one or more Facilitator acts and realize them. The coaching model will be based upon empirical studies of the CCC of effective repair strategies for conversing with persons with AD, as well as a study of particular syntactic forms used with specific strategies. This analysis makes great use of the necessary analysis about fluency and especially conversational repair strategies described in the previous section about NLU.

5 Summary

Co-constructed narrative between a person with DAT, and a skilled conversational partner offers a means by which persons with DAT and their caregivers may improve their social interaction and life satisfaction. Assistive technology can play a role in enabling even an unskilled conversational partner in maintaining the flow of the conversation. This paper presents an architecture for such a system, ASSIST, and describes how analysis of an existing corpus, the Carolinas Conversation Collection (CCC), can inform the development of the computational model for co-constructed narrative in ASSIST. We have begun preliminary analysis of excerpts from the CCC.

Acknowledgments

We gratefully acknowledge many years of encouragement and guidance from Dr. Boyd Davis, UNC Charlotte.

References

Allen, M., McGrenere, J., and Purves, B. (2008). The Field Evaluation of a Mobile Digital Image Communication Application Designed for People with Aphasia. *ACM Transactions on Accessible Computing*, Vol. 1, No. 1, Article 5.

Alm N., Dye, R., Gowans, G., Campbell, J., Astell, A. and Ellis, M. (2007). A communication support system for older people with dementia. *IEEE Computer,* May 2007: 35-41.

Alzheimer's Association. (2009). *2009 Alzheimer's Disease Facts and Figures.* Downloaded on 4/30/09 from www.alz.org.

Astell, A.J. et al. (2010). Using a touch screen computer to support relationships between people with dementia and caregivers. *Interacting with Computers*.

Bamberg, M. and Georgakopoulou, A. (2008). Small stories as a new perspective in narrative and identity analysis. *Text and Talk* 28(3): 377-396.

Bourgeois, M.S., Dijkstra, K., Burgio, L.D., and Allen, R.S. (2004). Communication Skills Training for Nursing Aides of Residents with Dementia: The Impact of Measuring Performance. *Clinical Gerontologist*, Vol. 27(1/2) 2004, 119-138.

Bucks, R., Singh, S., Cuerden, J.M., and G. Wilcock. (2000). Analysis of spontaneous, conversational speech in dementia of Alzheimer type: Evaluation of an objective technique for analyzing lexical performance, *Aphasiology*, vol. 14, no. 1, pp. 71-91.

Burgio, L.D., Allen-Burge, R., Roth, D.L., Bourgeois, M.S., Dijkstra, K., Gerstle, J., Jackson, E. and Bankester, L. (2001). Come talk with me: Improving communication between nursing assistants and nursing home residents during care routines. *The Gerontologist* 41: 449-460.

Burnside, I. (1996). Life Review and Reminiscence in Nursing Practice. In *Aging and Biography: Explorations in Adult Development*, Birren et al. (Eds.), Springer.

Callaway, C. (2000). *Narrative Prose Generation*. Ph.D. thesis, North Carolina State University, Raleigh, NC.

Cassell, J. (2004). Towards a model of technology and literacy development: Story listening systems. Applied Developmental Psychology 25: 75-105.

Cheepen, C. (1988). *The predictability of informal conversation.* Oxford: Printer Publishers Ltd.

Cherney, L.R., Shadden, B.B., and Coelho, C.A. (1998). *Analyzing Discourse in Communicatively Impaired Adults*. Aspen Publishers, Inc., Gaithersburg, Maryland.

Clark, H. H. and Schaefer, E.F.. Contributing to discourse. (1989). *Cognitive Science*, 13:259–294.

Coelho, C.A. (1998). Analysis of Story Grammar. In Cherney, L.R., Shadden, B.B., and Coelho, C.A. *Analyzing Discourse in Communicatively Impaired Adults*. Aspen Publishers, Inc., Gaithersburg, Maryland.

Cohene, T., Baecker, R., and Marziali, E. Designing Interactive Life Story Multimedia for a Family Affected by Alzheimer's Disease: A Case Study. *CHI 2005*, April 2–7, 2005, Portland, Oregon, USA., p.1300-1303.

Cosley, D., Akey, K., Alson, B., Baxter, J., Broomfield, M., Lee, S., and Sarabu, C. (2009). Using Technologies to Support Reminiscence. HCI 2009 – People and Computers XXIII – Celebrating people and technology, 480-484

Damianakis, T., Crete-Nishihata, Smith, K., Baecker, R.M., and Marziali, E. (2010). The psychosocial impacts of multimedia biographies on persons with cognitive impairments. *The Gerontologist* 50(1): 23-35.

Davis, B.H. (Ed.) (2005). *Alzheimer talk, text and context: Enhancing communication.* New York: Palgrave Macmillan.

Davis, B.H. (2010). Intentional stance and Lucinda Greystone. In V. Ramanathan and P. McPherron, eds. *Language, Bodies and Health.* NY: Continuum.

Davis, B.H. and Maclagan, M. (2009). Examining pauses in Alzheimer's discourse. *American Journal of Alzheimer's Disease and Other Dementias* 24, 141-154.

Davis, B.H. and Pope, C. (2009). Institutionalized ghosting: policy contexts and language use in erasing the person with Alzheimer's. *Language Policy.* Online First DOI 10.1007/s10993-009-9153-8.

Davis, B.H. and Smith, M. (2009). Infusing cultural competence training into the curriculum: Describing the development of culturally sensitive dementia care communication. *Kaohsiung Journal of Medical Sciences* 25, 503-510.

Dijkstra, K., Bourgeois, M., Allen, R., and Burgio, L. (2004). Conversational coherence: discourse analysis of older adults with and without dementia. *Journal of Neurolinguistics* 17: 263-283.

Elson, D.K. and McKeown, K.R. (2009). Extending and Evaluating a Platform for Story Understanding. *AAAI 2009 Spring Symposium on Intelligent Narrative Technologies II.*

Georgakopoulou, A. and Goutsos, D. (1997). *Discourse Analysis: An Introduction.* Edinburgh: Edinburgh University Press.

Green, N. (2002). A Virtual World for Coaching Caregivers of Persons with Alzheimer's Disease. *Papers from the AAAI Workshop on Automation as Caregiver: The Role of Intelligent Technology in Elder Care.* AAAI Press, Menlo Park, CA, pp. 18-23.

Green, N. (2005). Simulating Alzheimer's discourse for caregiver training in artificial intelligence-based dialogue systems. In Davis, Boyd H. (ed.). *Alzheimer talk, text and context: enhancing communication.* New York, NY: Palgrave Macmillan, 2005, 199-207.

Green, N and Bevan, C. (2009). Efficacy of Active Participation in Conversation with a Virtual Patient with Alzheimer's Disease. *Papers from 2009 AAAI Fall Symposium: Virtual Healthcare Interaction*, Arlington, Virginia from November 5- 7,2009.

Green, N. and B. Davis. (2003). Dialogue Generation in an Assistive Conversation Skills Training System for Caregivers of Persons with Alzheimer's Disease. In Papers from the 2003 AAAI Spring Symposium on Natural Language Generation in Spoken and Written Dialogue, pp. 36-43.

Green, N, Lawton, W., and Davis, B. (2004). An Assistive Conversation Skills Training System for Caregivers of Persons with Alzheimer's Disease. In *Proceedings of the AAAI 2004 Fall Symposium on Dialogue Systems for Health Communication.*

Guendouzi, J. and Muller, N. (2006). Approaches to discourse in dementia. Mahwah, NJ: Lawrence Erlbaum.

Halpin, H., Moore, J.D., and Robertson,J. (2004). Automatic Analysis of Plot for Story Rewriting. *Proceedings of Empirical Methods in Natural Language Processing.*

Hervás, R., Pereira, F., Gervás, P., andCardoso, A. (2006) Cross-domain analogy in automated text generation, Proc. of the Third joint workshop on Computational Creativity, ECAI'06, Trento, Italy.

Hsieh, H.F. Effect of reminiscence therapy on depression in older adults: a systematic review. (2003). *International Journal of Nursing Studies*, 40(4):335–345.

Irvine, A.B., Ary, D.V., and Bourgeois, M.S. (2003). An Interactive Multimedia Program to Train Professional Caregivers. *Journal of Applied Gerontology* 22(2), June 2003, 269-288.

Labov, W. (1972). *Language in the inner city.* Philadelphia: University of Pennsylvania Press.

Lenchuk, I. and M. Swain. (2010). Alise's small stories: indices of identity construction and of resistance to the discourse of cognitive impairment. *Language Policy* : 9-28.

Martin, A. and P. Fedio, (1983). Word production and comprehension in Alzheimer's disease: The breakdown of semantic knowledge, Brain and Language, Volume 19, Issue 1, May 1983, Pages 124-141.

Massimi, M., Berry, E., Browne, G., Smyth, G., Watson, P., and Baecker, R. M. (2008). *Neuropsychological Rehabilitation* 18(5-6): 742-765.

McCallion, P., Toseland, R.W., Lacey, D., and Banks, S. (1999). Educating nursing assistants to communicate more effectively with nursing home residents with dementia. *The Gerontologist* 39(5): 546-558.

Moore, L. & B. Davis. (2002) Quilting narrative: using repetition techniques to help elderly communicators. *Geriatric Nursing,* 23(5):262-6.

Orange, J. B. (2001). Family caregivers, communication, and Alzheimer's disease. In M. L. Hummert & J. F. Nussbaum (Eds.), *Aging communication, and health: Linking research and practice for successful aging* (pp. 225-248). Mahwah, NJ: Lawrence Eribaum Associates, Inc.

Passonneau,R., Goodkind, A., and Levy, E. (2007). Annotation of children's oral narrations: Modeling emergent narrative skills for computational applications. *Proceedings of the 20th Annual Meeting of the Florida Artificial Intelligence Research Society (FLAIRS-20).*

Petrelli, D., van den Hoven, E., and Whittaker, S. (2009). Making history: Intentional capture of future memories. CHI 2009, April 4-9, 2009, Boston, MA. pp. 1723-1732.

Phillips, L., Sala, S.D. and C. Trivelli. (1996). Fluency deficits in patients with Alzheimer's disease and frontal lobe lesions, *European Journal of Neurology*, vol. 3, pp. 102.108.

Piwek, P. and S. Stoyanchev (2010). Generating Expository Dialogue from Monologue: Motivation, Corpus and Preliminary Rules. NAACL HLT 2010.

Polanyi , L. (1985). *Telling the American Story: A Structural and Cultural Analysis of Conversational Storytelling*. Norwood, NJ: Ablex.

Polkinghorne, D.E. (1996). Narrative Knowing and the Study of Lives. In Aging and biography: explorations in adult development, Birren, J.E., Kenyon, G.M., Ruth, J., Schroots, J.J.F., and Svensson, T. (Eds.), Springer.

Pope, C. and Davis, B.H. (2011). Finding a balance: The Carolinas Conversation Collection. *Corpus Linguistics and Linguistic Theory* 7-1, 143-161.

Ramanathan V. (1997). *Alzheimer Discourse: Some Sociolinguistic Dimensions.* Mahwah, NJ: Lawrence Erlbaum.

Ripich, D.N., Ziol, E., and Lee, M.M. (1998). Longitudinal Effects of Communication Training on Caregivers of Persons with Alzheimer's Disease. *Clinical Gerontologist* 19(2): 37-55.

Roark, B., Fowler, A., Sproat, R., Gibbons, C., and Fried-Oken, M. 2011. Towards technology-assisted co-construction with communication partners. *Proceedings of the 2nd Workshop on Speech and Language Processing for Assistive Technologies.* pp. 22-31.

Ryokai, K., Vaucelle, C. and Cassell, J. 2003. Virtual peers as partners in storytelling and literacy learning. *Journal of Computer Assisted Learning*, 19(2), 195-208.

Sabat, S. (1994). Language function in Alzheimer's disease: a critical review of selected literature, *Language and Communication*, vol. 14, pp. 331-351.

Santo Pietro, Mary Jo and Ostuni, Elizabeth. (2003). *Successful Communication with Persons with Alzheimer's Disease, An In-Service Manual*, 2nd ed., Butterworth Heinemann, St. Louis, Missouri.

Shenk, D., Davis, B., Peacock, J. and L. Moore. (2002). Narratives and self-identity in later life: Two rural American older women, *Journal of Aging Studies*, Volume 16, Issue 4, November 2002, Pages 401-413.

Singh, S. and T. Bookless. (1997).Analyzing Spontaneous Speech in Dysphasic Adults, *International Journal of Applied Linguistics*, vol. 7.2, no. 2, pp. 165-182.

Smith, J. (2000). *GrandChair: Conversational collection of family stories*. Media Arts and Sciences. Unpublished master's thesis, MIT, Cambridge, MA.

Smith, K.L., Crete-Nishihata, M., Damianakis, T., Baecker,R.M., and Marziali, E. (2009). Multimedia biographies: a reminiscence and social stimulus tool for persons with cognitive impairment. *Journal of Technology in Human Services,* 27(4): 287-306.

Smith, M., Davis B., et al. (2010). Twelve important minutes: Introducing enhanced online materials about elder abuse to Nursing Assistants. *Journal of Continuing Education for Nursing.*

Theune, M., Slabbers, N., and Hielkema, F. (2007). The Narrator: NLG for digital storytelling. Proc ENLG 07, 109-112.

Traum, D. R. (1994). *A Computational Theory of Grounding in Natural Language Conversation*. PhD thesis, Department of Computer Science, University of Rochester, Also available as TR 545, Department of Computer Science, University of Rochester.

Waller, A. (2006). Communication Access to Conversational Narrative. *Topics in Language Disorders* 26(3): 221-239.

Wiebe, J., Wilson, T., and Cardie, C. (2005). Annotating expressions of opinions and emotions in language, *Language Resources and Evaluation*, 1(2): 165-210.

Woods, B., Spector, A., Jones, C., Orrell,M., and Davies, S. (2005). Reminiscence therapy for dementia.*Cochrane Database of Systematic Reviews.*

Communication strategies for a computerized caregiver for individuals with Alzheimer's disease

Frank Rudzicz[1,2,] * and **Rozanne Wilson**[1] and **Alex Mihailidis**[2] and **Elizabeth Rochon**[1]
[1] Department of Speech-Language Pathology,
[2] Department of Occupational Science and Occupational Therapy
University of Toronto
Toronto Canada

Carol Leonard
School of Rehabilitation Sciences
University of Ottawa
Ottawa Canada

Abstract

Currently, health care costs associated with aging at home can be prohibitive if individuals require continual or periodic supervision or assistance because of Alzheimer's disease. These costs, normally associated with human caregivers, can be mitigated to some extent given automated systems that mimic some of their functions. In this paper, we present inaugural work towards producing a generic automated system that assists individuals with Alzheimer's to complete daily tasks using verbal communication. Here, we show how to improve rates of correct speech recognition by preprocessing acoustic noise and by modifying the vocabulary according to the task. We conclude by outlining current directions of research including specialized grammars and automatic detection of confusion.

1 Introduction

In the United States, approximately $100 billion are spent annually on the direct and indirect care of individuals with Alzheimer's disease (AD), the majority of which is attributed to long-term institutional care (Ernst et al., 1997). As the population ages, the incidence of AD will double or triple, with Medicare costs alone reaching $189 billion in the US by 2015 (Bharucha et al., 2009). Given the growing need to support this population, there is an increasing interest in the design and development of technologies that support this population at home and extend ones quality of life and autonomy (Mihailidis et al., 2008).

Alzheimer's disease is a type of progressive neuro-degenerative dementia characterized by marked declines in mental acuity, specifically in cognitive, social, and functional capacity. A decline in memory (short- and long-term), executive capacity, visual-spacial reasoning, and linguistic ability are all typical effects of AD (Cummings, 2004). These declines make the completion of activities of daily living (e.g., finances, preparing a meal) difficult and more severe declines often necessitate caregiver assistance. Caregivers who assist individuals with AD at home are common, but are often the precursor to placement in a long-term care (LTC) facility (Gaugler et al., 2009).

We are building systems that automate, where possible, some of the support activities that currently require family or formal (i.e., employed) caregivers. Specifically, we are designing an intelligent dialog component that can engage in two-way speech communication with an individual in order to help guide that individual towards the completion of certain daily household tasks, including washing ones hands and brushing ones teeth. A typical installation setup in a bathroom, shown in figure 1, consists of video cameras that track a user's hands and the area in and around the sink, as well as microphones, speakers, and a screen that can display prompting information. Similar installations are being tested in other household rooms as part of the COACH project (Mihailidis et al., 2008), according to the task; this is an example of ambient intelligence in which technology embedded in the environment is sensitive to the activities of the user with it (Spanoudakis et al., 2010).

*Contact: frank@cs.toronto.edu

Our goal is to encode in software the kinds of techniques used by caregivers to help their clients achieve these activities; this includes automatically identifying and recovering from breakdowns in communication and flexibly adapting to the individual over time. Before such a system can be deployed, the underlying models need to be adjusted to the desired population and tasks. Similarly, the speech output component would need to be programmed according to the vocabularies, grammars, and dialog strategies used by caregivers. This paper presents preliminary experiments towards dedicated speech recognition for such a system. Evaluation data were collected as part of a larger project examining the use of communication strategies by formal caregivers while assisting residents with moderate to severe AD during the completion of toothbrushing (Wilson et al., 2012).

2 Background – communication strategies

Automated communicative systems that are more sensitive to the emotive and the mental states of their users are often more successful than more neutral conversational agents (Saini et al., 2005). In order to be useful in practice, these communicative systems need to mimic some of the techniques employed by caregivers of individuals with AD. Often, these caregivers are employed by local clinics or medical institutions and are trained by those institutions in ideal verbal *communication strategies* for use with those having dementia (Hopper, 2001; Goldfarb and Pietro, 2004). These include (Small et al., 2003) but are not limited to:

1. Relatively slow rate of speech rate.
2. Verbatim repetition of misunderstood prompts.
3. Closed-ended questions (i.e., that elicit yes/no responses).
4. Simple sentences with reduced syntactic complexity.
5. Giving one question or one direction at a time.
6. Minimal use of pronouns.

These strategies, though often based on observational studies, are not necessarily based on quantitative empirical research and may not be generalizable across relevant populations. Indeed, Tomoeda et al. (1990) showed that rates of speech that are too slow

(a) Environmental setup

(b) On-screen prompting

Figure 1: Setup and on-screen prompting for COACH. The environment includes numerous sensors including microphones and video cameras as well as a screen upon which prompts can be displayed. In this example, the user is prompted to lather their hands after having applied soap. Images are copyright Intelligent Assistive Technology and Systems Lab).

may interfere with comprehension if they introduce

problems of short-term retention of working memory. Small, Andersen, and Kempler (1997) showed that paraphrased repetition is just as effective as verbatim repetition (indeed, syntactic variation of common semantics may assist comprehension). Furthermore, Rochon, Waters, and Caplan (2000) suggested that the syntactic complexity of utterances is not necessarily the only predictor of comprehension in individuals with AD; rather, correct comprehension of the semantics of sentences is inversely related to the increasing number of propositions used – it is preferable to have as few clauses or core ideas as possible, i.e., one-at-a-time.

Although not the empirical subject of this paper, we are studying methods of automating the resolution of communication breakdown. Much of this work is based on the Trouble Source-Repair (TSR) model in which difficulties in speaking, hearing, or understanding are identified and repairs are initiated and carried out (Schegloff, Jefferson, and Sacks, 1977). Difficulties can arise in a number of dimensions including phonological (i.e., mispronunciation), morphological/syntactic (e.g., incorrect agreement among constituents), semantic (e.g., disturbances related to lexical access, word retrieval, or word use), and discourse (i.e., misunderstanding of topic, shared knowledge, or cohesion) (Orange, Lubinsky, and Higginbotham, 1996). The majority of TSR sequences involve self-correction of a speaker's own error, e.g., by repetition, elaboration, or reduction of a troublesome utterance (Schegloff, Jefferson, and Sacks, 1977). Orange, Lubinsky, and Higginbotham (1996) showed that while 18% of non-AD dyad utterances involved TSR, whereas 23.6% of early-stage AD dyads and 33% of middle-stage AD dyads involved TSR. Of these, individuals with middle-stage AD exhibited more discourse-related difficulties including inattention, failure to track propositions and thematic information, and deficits in working memory. The most common repair initiators and repairs given communication breakdown involved frequent '*wh*-questions and hypotheses (e.g., "*Do you mean?*"). Conversational partners of individuals with middle-stage AD initiated repair less frequently than conversational partners of control subjects, possibly aware of their deteriorating ability, or to avoid possible further confusion. An alternative although very closely related paradigm for measuring communication breakdown is Trouble Indicating Behavior (TIB) in which the confused participant implicitly or explicitly requests aid. In a study of 7 seniors with moderate/severe dementia and 3 with mild/moderate dementia, Watson (1999) showed that there was a significant difference in TIB use ($\rho < 0.005$) between individuals with AD and the general population. Individuals with AD are most likely to exhibit dysfluency, lack of uptake in the dialog, metalinguistic comments (e.g., "*I can't think of the word*"), neutral requests for repetition, whereas the general population are most likely to exhibit hypothesis formation to resolve ambiguity (e.g., "*Oh, so you mean that you had a good time?*") or requests for more information.

2.1 The task of handwashing

Our current work is based on a study completed by Wilson et al. (2012) towards a systematic observational representation of communication behaviours of formal caregivers assisting individuals with moderate to severe AD during hand washing. In that study, caregivers produced 1691 utterances, 78% of which contained at least one communication strategy. On average, 23.35 ($\sigma = 14.11$) verbal strategies and 7.81 ($\sigma = 5.13$) non-verbal strategies were used per session. The five most common communication strategies employed by caregivers are ranked in table 1. The *one proposition* strategy refers to using a single direction, request, or idea in the utterance (e.g. "turn the water on"). The *closed-ended question* strategy refers to asking question with a very limited, typically binary, response (e.g., "can you turn the taps on?") as opposed to questions eliciting a more elaborate response or the inclusion of additional information. The *encouraging comments* strategy refers to any verbal praise of the resident (e.g., "you are doing a good job"). The *paraphrased repetition* strategy is the restatement of a misunderstood utterance using alternative syntactic or lexical content (e.g., "soap up your hands....please use soap on your hands"). There was no significant difference between the use of paraphrased and verbatim repetition of misunderstood utterances. Caregivers also reduced speech rate from an average baseline of 116 words per minute (s.d. 36.8) to an average of 36.5 words per minute (s.d. 19.8).

The least frequently used communication strate-

Verbal strategy	Number of occurrences Overall	Successful	% use of strategy Overall	Successful	Uses per session Mean	SD
One proposition	619	441	35	36	8.6	6.7
Closed-ended question	215	148	12	12	3.0	3.0
Encouraging comments	180	148	10	12	2.9	2.5
Use of resident's name	178	131	10	11	2.8	2.5
Paraphrased repetition	178	122	10	10	3.0	2.5

Table 1: Most frequent verbal communication strategies according to their number of occurrences in dyad communication. The % use of strategy is normalized across all strategies, most of which are not listed. These results are split according to the total number of uses and the number of uses in successful resolution of a communication breakdown. Mean (and standard deviation) of uses per session are given across caregivers. Adapted with permission from Wilson et al. (2012).

gies employed by experienced caregivers involved asking questions that required verification of a resident's request or response (e.g., "do you mean that you are finished?"), explanation of current actions (e.g., "I am turning on the taps for you"), and open-ended questions (e.g., "how do you wash your hands?").

The most common non-verbal strategies employed by experienced caregivers were *guided touch* (193 times, 122 of which were successful) in which the caregiver physically assists the resident in the completion of a task, *demonstrating action* (113 times. 72 of which were successful) in which an action is illustrated or mimicked by the caregiver, *handing an object to the resident* (107 times, 85 of which were successful), and *pointing to an object* (105 times, 95 of which were successful) in which the direction to an object is visually indicated by the caregiver. Some of these strategies may be employed by the proposed system; for example, videos demonstrating an action may be displayed on the screen shown in figure 1(a), which may replace to some extent the mimicry by the caregiver. A possible replication of the fourth most common non-verbal strategy may be to highlight the required object with a flashing light, a spotlight, or by displaying it on screen; these solutions require tangential technologies that are beyond the scope of this current study, however.

3 Data

Our experiments are based on data collected by Wilson et al. (submitted) with individuals diagnosed with moderate-to-severe AD who were recruited from long-term care facilities (i.e., The Harold and Grace Baker Centre and the Lakeside Long-Term Care Centre) in Toronto. Participants had no previous history of stroke, depression, psychosis, alcoholism, drug abuse, or physical aggression towards caregivers. Updated measures of disease severity were taken according to the Mini-Mental State Examination (Folstein, Folstein, and McHugh, 1975). The average cognitive impairment among 7 individuals classified as having severe AD (scores below $10/30$) was 3.43 ($\sigma = 3.36$) and among 6 individuals classified as having moderate AD (scores between $10/30$ and $19/30$) was 15.8 ($\sigma = 4.07$). The average age of residents was 81.4 years with an average of 13.8 years of education and 3.1 years of residency at their respective LTC facility. Fifteen formal caregivers participated in this study and were paired with the residents (i.e., as dyads) during the completion of activities of daily living. All but one caregiver were female and were comfortable with English. The average number of years of experience working with AD patients was 12.87 ($\sigma = 9.61$).

The toothbrushing task follows the protocol of the handwashing task. In total, the data consists of 336 utterances by the residents and 2623 utterances by their caregivers; this is manifested by residents uttering 1012 words and caregivers uttering 12166 words in total, using 747 unique terms. The toothbrushing task consists of 9 subtasks, namely: 1) get brush and paste, 2) put paste on brush, 3) turn on water, 4) wet tooth brush, 5) brush teeth, 6) rinse mouth, 7) rinse brush, 8) turn off water, 9) dry mouth.

These data were recorded as part of a large project to study communication strategies of caregivers rather than to study the acoustics of their transactions with residents. As a result, the recordings were not of the highest acoustic quality; for example, although the sampling rate and bit rate were high (48 kHz and 384 kbps respectively), the video camera used was placed relatively far from the speakers, who generally faced away from the microphone towards the sink and running water. The distribution of strategies employed by caregivers for this task is the subject of ongoing work.

4 Experiments in speech recognition

Our first component of an automated caregiver is the speech recognition subsystem. We test two alternative systems, namely Carnegie Mellon's Sphinx framework and Microsoft's Speech Platform. Carnegie Mellon's Sphinx framework (pocketsphinx, specifically) is an open-source speech recognition system that uses traditional N-gram language modeling, sub-phonetic acoustic hidden Markov models (HMMs), Viterbi decoding and lexical-tree structures (Lamere et al., 2003). Sphinx includes tools to perform traditional Baum-Welch estimation of acoustic models, but there were not enough data for this purpose. The second ASR system, Microsoft's Speech Platform (version 11) is less open but exposes the ability to vary the lexicon, grammar, and semantics. Traditionally, Microsoft has used continuous-density HMMs with 6000 tied HMM states (senones), 20 Gaussians per state, and Mel-cepstrum features (with delta and delta-delta).

Given the toothbrushing data described in section 3, two sets of experiments were devised to configure these systems to the task. Specifically, we perform preprocessing of the acoustics to remove environmental noise associated with toothbrushing and adapt the lexica of the two systems, as described in the following subsections.

4.1 Noise reduction

An emergent feature of the toothbrushing data is very high levels of acoustic noise caused by the running of water. In fact, the estimated signal-to-noise ratio across utterances range from -2.103 dB to 7.63 dB, which is extremely low; for comparison clean speech typically has an SNR of approximately 40 dB. Since the resident is likely to be situated close to this source of the acoustic noise, it becomes important to isolate their speech in the incoming signal.

Speech enhancement involves the removal of acoustic noise $d(t)$ in a signal $y(t)$, including ambient noise (e.g., running water, wind) and signal degradation giving the clean 'source' signal $x(t)$. This involves an assumption that noise is strictly additive, as in the formula:

$$y(t) = x(t) + d(t). \tag{1}$$

Here, Y_k, X_k, and D_k are the kth spectra of the noisy observation $y(t)$, source signal $x(t)$, and uncorrelated noise signal $d(t)$, respectively. Generally, the spectral magnitude of a signal is more important than its phase when assessing signal quality and performing speech enhancement. Spectral subtraction (SS), as the name suggests, subtracts an estimate of the noisy spectrum from the measured signal (Boll, 1979; Martin, 2001), where the estimate of the noisy signal is estimated from samples of the noise source exclusively. That is, one has to learn estimates based on pre-selected recordings of noise. We apply SS speech enhancement given sample recordings of water running. The second method of enhancement we consider is the log-spectral amplitude estimator (LSAE) which minimizes the mean squared error (MMSE) of the log spectra given a model for the source speech $X_k = A_k \exp(j\omega_k)$, where A_k is the spectral amplitude. The LSAE method is a modification to the short-time spectral amplitude estimator that attempts to find some estimate $\hat{A}_k$ that minimizes the distortion

$$E\left[\left(logA_k - \log \hat{A}_k\right)^2\right], \tag{2}$$

such that the log-spectral amplitude estimate is

$$\begin{aligned} \hat{A}_k &= \exp\left(E\left[\ln A_k \mid Y_k\right]\right) \\ &= \frac{\xi_k}{1+\xi_k} \exp\left(\frac{1}{2}\int_{v_k}^{\infty} \frac{e^{-t}}{t} dt\right) R_k, \end{aligned} \tag{3}$$

where ξ_k is the *a priori* SNR, R_k is the noisy spectral amplitude, $v_k = \frac{\xi_k}{1+\xi_k}\gamma_k$, and γ_k is the *a posteriori* SNR (Erkelens, Jensen, and Heusdens, 2007). Often this is based on a Gaussian model of noise, as it is here (Ephraim and Malah, 1985). We enhance our recordings by both the SS and LSAE methods. Archetypal instances of typical, low, and (relatively) high SNR waveform recordings and their enhanced versions are shown in 4.1.

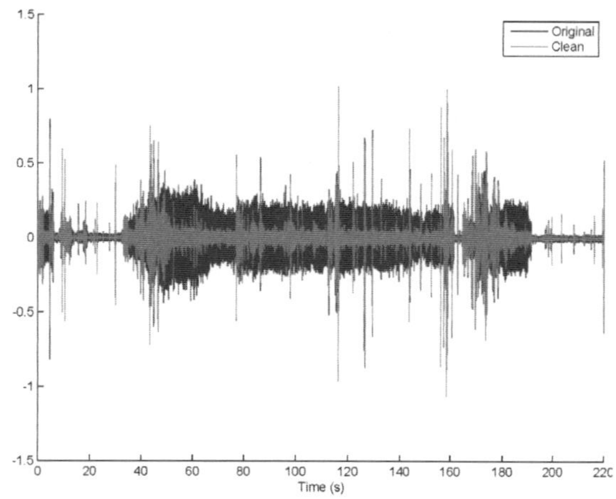

(a) Dyad1.1

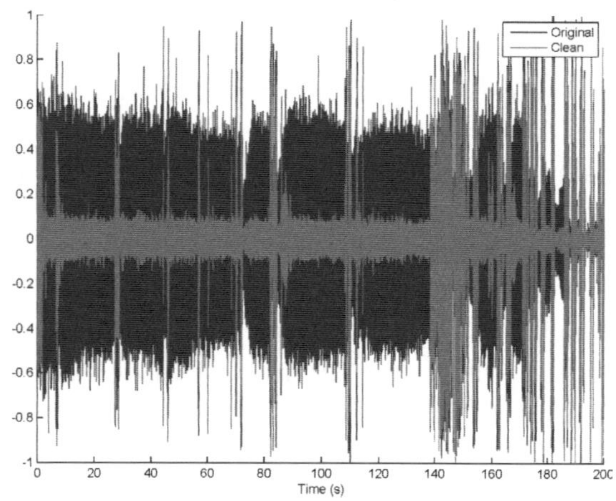

(b) Dyad4.2

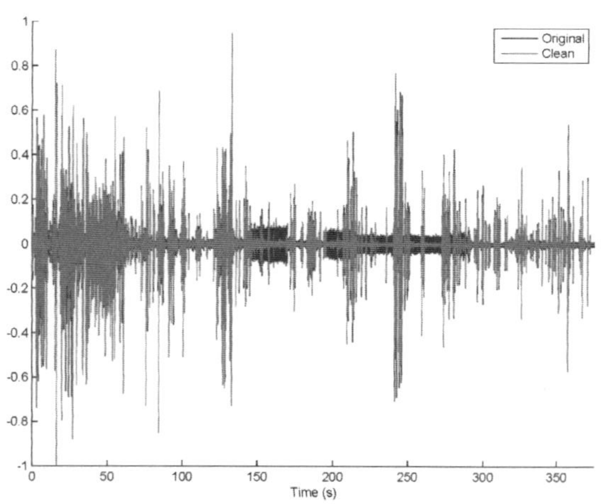

(c) Dyad11.1

Figure 2: Representative samples of toothbrushing data audio. Figures show normalized amplitude over time for signals cleaned by the LSAE method overlaid over the larger-amplitude original signals.

We compare the effects of this enhanced audio across two ASR systems. For the Sphinx system, we use a continuous tristate HMM for each of the 40 phones from the CMU dictionary trained with audio from the complete Wall Street Journal corpus and the independent variable we changed was the number of Gaussians per state (n. Γ). These parameters are not exposed by the Microsoft speech system, so we instead vary the minimum threshold of confidence $\mathcal{C} \in [0..1]$ required to accept a word; in theory lower values of $\mathcal{C}$ would result in more insertion errors and higher values would result in more deletion errors. For each system, we used a common dictionary of $123,611$ unique words derived from the Carnegie Mellon phonemic dictionary.

Table 2 shows the word error rate for each of the two systems. Both the SS and LSAE methods of speech enhancement result in significantly better word error rates than with the original recordings at the 99.9% level of confidence according to the one-tailed paired t-test across both systems. The LSAE method has significantly better word error rates than the SS method at the 99% level of confidence with this test. Although these high WERs are impractical for a typical system, they are comparable to other results for speech recognition in very low-SNR environments (Kim and Rose, 2003). Deng et al. (2000), for example, describe an ASR system trained with clean speech that has a WER of 87.11% given additive white noise for a resulting 5 dB SNR signal for a comparable vocabulary of 5000 words. An interesting observation is that even at the low confidence threshold of $\mathcal{C} = 0.2$, the number of insertion errors did not increase dramatically relative to for the higher values in the Microsoft system; only 4.0% of all word errors were insertion errors at $\mathcal{C} = 0.2$, and 2.7% of all word errors at $\mathcal{C} = 0.8$.

Given Levenshtein alignments between annotated target (reference) and hypothesis word sequences, we separate word errors across residents and across caregivers. Specifically, table 3 shows the proportion of deletion and substitution word errors (relative to totals for each system separately) across residents and caregivers. This analysis aims to uncover differences in rates of recognition between those with AD and the more general population. For example, 12.6% of deletion errors made by Sphinx were words spoken by residents. It is not possible to at-

	Parameters	Word error rate % Original	SS	LSAE
Sphinx	n. $\Gamma = 4$	98.13	75.31	70.61
	n. $\Gamma = 8$	98.13	74.95	69.66
	n. $\Gamma = 16$	97.82	75.09	69.78
	n. $\Gamma = 32$	97.13	74.88	67.22
Microsoft	$\mathcal{C} = 0.8$	97.67	73.59	67.11
	$\mathcal{C} = 0.6$	97.44	72.57	67.08
	$\mathcal{C} = 0.4$	96.85	71.78	66.54
	$\mathcal{C} = 0.2$	94.30	71.36	64.32

Table 2: Word error rates for the Sphinx and Microsoft ASR systems according to their respective adjusted parameters, i.e., number of Gaussians per HMM state (n. Γ) and minimum confidence threshold ($\mathcal{C}$). Results are given on original recordings and waveforms enhanced by spectral subraction (SS) and MMSE with log-spectral amplitude estimates (LSAE).

tribute word insertion errors to either the resident or caregiver, in general. If we assume that errors should be distributed across residents and caregivers in the same proportion as their respective total number of words uttered, then we can compute the Pearson χ^2 statistic of significance. Given that 7.68% of all words were uttered by residents, the observed number of substitutions was significantly different than the expected value at the 99% level of confidence for both the Sphinx and Microsoft systems, but the number of deletions was not significantly different even at the 95% level of confidence. In either case, however, substantially more errors are made proportionally by residents than we might expect; this may in part be caused by their relatively soft speech.

	Proportion of errors Sphinx Res.	Careg.	Microsoft Res.	Careg.
deletion	13.9	86.1	12.6	87.4
substitution	23.2	76.8	18.4	81.6

Table 3: Proportion of deletion and substitution errors made by both (Res)idents and (Careg)ivers. Proportions are relative to totals within each system.

4.2 Task-specific vocabulary

We limit the common vocabulary used in each speech recognizer in order to be more specific to the task. Specifically, we begin with the 747 words uttered in the data as our most restricted vocabulary. Then, we expand this vocabulary according to two methods. The first method adds words that are semantically similar to those already present. This is performed by taking the most common sense for each noun, verb, adjective, and adverb, then adding each entry in the respective synonym sets according to WordNet 3.0 (Miller, 1995). This results in a vocabulary of 2890 words. At this point, we iteratively add increments of words at intervals of $10,000$ (up to $120,000$) by selecting random words in the vocabulary and adding synonym sets for all senses as well as antonyms, hypernyms, hyponyms, meronyms, and holonyms. The result is a vocabulary whose semantic domain becomes increasingly generic. The second approach to adjusting the vocabulary size is to add phonemic foils to more restricted vocabularies. Specifically, as before, we begin with the restricted 747 words observed in the data but then add increments of new words that are phonemically similar to existing words. This is done exhaustively by selecting a random word and searching for minimal phonemic misalignments (i.e., edit distance) among out-of-vocabulary words in the Carnegie Mellon phonemic dictionary. This approach of adding decoy words is an attempt to model increasing generalization of the systems. Every vocabulary is translated into the format expected by each recognizer so that each test involves a common set of words.

Word error rates are measured for each vocabulary size across each ASR system and the manner in which those vocabularies were constructed (semantic or phonemic expansion). The results are shown in figure 4.2 and are based on acoustics enhanced by the LSAE method. Somewhat surprisingly, the method used to alter the vocabulary did appear to have a very large effect. Indeed, the WER across the semantic and phonemic methods were correlated at $\rho >= 0.99$ across both ASR systems; there was no significant difference between traces (within system) even at the 60% level of confidence using the two-tailed heteroscedastic t-test.

5 Ongoing work

This work represents the first phase of development towards a complete communicative artificial caregiver for the home. Here, we are focusing on the

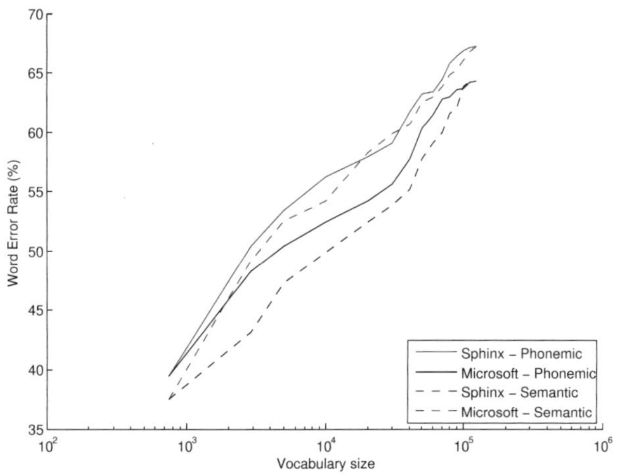

Figure 3: Word error rate versus size of vocabulary (log scale) for each of the Sphinx and Microsoft ASR systems according to whether the vocabularies were expanded by semantic or phonemic similarity.

speech recognition component and have shown reductions in error of up to 72% (Sphinx ASR with $n.\Gamma = 4$) and 63.1% (Sphinx ASR), relative to baseline rates of error. While significant, baseline errors were so severe that other techniques will need to be explored. We are now collecting additional data by fixing the Microsoft Kinect sensor in the environment, facing the resident; this is the default configuration and may overcome some of the obstacles present in our data. Specifically, the beamforming capabilities in the Kinect (generalizable to other multi-microphone arrays) can isolate speech events from ambient environmental noise (Balan and Rosca, 2002). We are also collecting speech data for a separate study in which individuals with AD are placed before directional microphones and complete tasks related to the perception of emotion.

As tasks can be broken down into non-linear (partially ordered) sets of subtasks (e.g., replacing the toothbrush is a subtask of toothbrushing), we are specifying grammars 'by hand' specific to those subtasks. Only some subset of all subtasks are possible at any given time; e.g., one can only place toothpaste on the brush once both items have been retrieved. The possibility of these subtasks depend on the state of the world which can only be estimated through imperfect techniques – typically computer vision. Given the uncertainty of the state of the world, we are integrating subtask-specific grammars into a partially-observable Markov decision process (POMDP). These grammars include the semantic state variables of the world and break each task down into a graph-structure of interdependent actions. Each 'action' is associated with its own grammar subset of words and phrases that are likely to be uttered during its performance, as well as a set of prompts to be spoken by the system to aid the user. Along these lines, we we will attempt to generalize the approach taken in section 4.2 to generate specific sub-vocabularies automatically for each subtask. The relative weighting of words will be modeled based on ongoing data collection.

Acknowledgments

This research was partially funded by Mitacs and an operating grant from the Canadian Institutes of Health Research and the American Alzheimer Association (ETAC program). The authors acknowledge and thank the administrative staff, caregivers, and residents at the Harold and Grace Baker Centre and the Lakeside Long-Term Care Centre.

References

Balan, Radu and Justinian Rosca. 2002. Microphone Array Speech Enhancement by Bayesian Estimation of Spectral Amplitude and Phase. In *Proceedings of IEEE Sensor Array and Multichannel Signal Processing Workshop*.

Bharucha, Ashok J., Vivek Anand, Jodi Forlizzi, Mary Amanda Dew, Charles F. Reynolds III, Scott Stevens, and Howard Wactlar. 2009. Intelligent assistive technology applications to dementia care: Current capabilities, limitations, and future challenges. *American Journal of Geriatric Psychiatry*, 17(2):88–104, February.

Boll, S.F. 1979. Suppression of acoustic noise in speech using spectral subtraction. *IEEE Transactions on Acoustics, Speech, and Signal Processing*, 27(2):113–120, April.

Cummings, Jeffrey L. 2004. Alzheimer's disease. *New England Journal of Medicine*, 351(1):56–67.

Deng, Li, Alex Acero, M. Plumpe, and Xuedong Huang. 2000. Large-vocabulary speech recognition under adverse acoustic environments. In *Proceedings of the International Conference on Spoken Language Processing*, October.

Ephraim, Y. and D. Malah. 1985. Speech enhancement using a minimum mean-square error log-spectral amplitude estimator. *Acoustics, Speech and Signal Processing, IEEE Transactions on*, 33(2):443 – 445, apr.

Erkelens, Jan, Jesper Jensen, and Richard Heusdens. 2007. A data-driven approach to optimizing spectral speech enhancement methods for various error criteria. *Speech Communication*, 49:530–541.

Ernst, Richard L., Joel W. Hay, Catharine Fenn, Jared Tinklenberg, and Jerome A. Yesavage. 1997. Cognitive function and the costs of alzheimer disease – an exploratory study. *Archives of Neurology*, 54:687–693.

Folstein, Marshal F., Susan E. Folstein, and Paul R. McHugh. 1975. Mini-mental state: A practical method for grading the cognitive state of patients for the clinician. *Journal of Psychiatric Research*, 12(3):189–198, November.

Gaugler, J. E., F. Yu, K. Krichbaum, and J.F. Wyman. 2009. Predictors of nursing home admission for persons with dementia. *Medical Care*, 47(2):191–198.

Goldfarb, R. and M.J.S. Pietro. 2004. Support systems: Older adults with neurogenic communication disorders. *Journal of Ambulatory Care Management*, 27(4):356–365.

Hopper, T. 2001. Indirect interventions to facilitate communication in Alzheimers disease. *Seminars in Speech and Language*, 22(4):305–315.

Kim, Hong Kook and Richard C. Rose. 2003. Cepstrum-Domain Acoustic Feature Compensation Based on Decomposition of Speech and Noise for ASR in Noisy Environments. *IEEE Transactions on Speech and Audio Processing*, 11(5), September.

Lamere, Paul, Philip Kwok, Evandro Gouvea, Bhiksha Raj, Rita Singh, William Walker, M. Warmuth, and Peter Wolf. 2003. The CMU Sphinx-4 speech recognition system. In *IEEE International Conference on Acoustics, Speech, and Signal Processing (ICASSP 2003)*, Hong Kong, April.

Martin, Rainer. 2001. Noise power spectral density estimation based on optimal smoothing and minimum statistics. *IEEE Transactions of Speech and Audio Processing*, 9(5):504–512, July.

Mihailidis, Alex, Jennifer N Boger, Tammy Craig, and Jesse Hoey. 2008. The COACH prompting system to assist older adults with dementia through handwashing: An efficacy study. *BMC Geriatrics*, 8(28).

Miller, George A. 1995. WordNet: A Lexical Database for English. *Communications of the ACM*, 38(11):39–41.

Orange, J.B., Rosemary B. Lubinsky, and D. Jeffery Higginbotham. 1996. Conversational repair by individuals with dementia of the alzheimer's type. *Journal of Speech and Hearing Research*, 39:881–895, August.

Rochon, Elizabeth, Gloria S. Waters, and David Caplan. 2000. The Relationship Between Measures of Working Memory and Sentence Comprehension in Patients With Alzheimer's Disease. *Journal of Speech, Language, and Hearing Research*, 43:395–413.

Saini, Privender, Boris de Ruyter, Panos Markopoulos, and Albert van Breemen. 2005. Benefits of social intelligence in home dialogue systems. In *Proceedings of INTERACT 2005*, pages 510–521.

Schegloff, Emanuel A., Gail Jefferson, and Harvey Sacks. 1977. The preference for self-correction in the organization of repair in conversation. *1977*, 53(2):361–382.

Small, Jeff A., Elaine S. Andersen, and Daniel Kempler. 1997. Effects of working memory capacity on understanding rate-altered speech. *Aging, Neuropsychology, and Cognition*, 4(2):126–139.

Small, Jeff A., Gloria Gutman, Saskia Makela, and Beth Hillhouse. 2003. Effectiveness of communication strategies used by caregivers of persons with alzheimer's disease during activities of daily living. *Journal of Speech, Language, and Hearing Research*, 46(2):353–367.

Spanoudakis, Nikolaos, Boris Grabner, Christina Kotsiopoulou, Olga Lymperopoulou, Verena Moser-Siegmeth, Stylianos Pantelopoulos, Paraskevi Sakka, and Pavlos Moraitis. 2010. A novel architecture and process for ambient assisted living - the hera approach. In *Proceedings of the 10th IEEE International Conference on Information Technology and Applications in Biomedicine (ITAB)*, pages 1–4.

Tomoeda, Cheryl K., Kathryn A. Bayles, Daniel R. Boone, Alfred W. Kaszniak, and Thomas J. Slauson. 1990. Speech rate and syntactic complexity effects on the auditory comprehension of alzheimer patients. *Journal of Communication Disorders*, 23(2):151 – 161.

Watson, Caroline M. 1999. An analysis of trouble and repair in the natural conversations of people with dementia of the Alzheimer's type. *Aphasiology*, 13(3):195 – 218.

Wilson, Rozanne, Elizabeth Rochon, Alex Mihailidis, and Carol Léonard. 2012. Examining success of communication strategies used by formal caregivers assisting individuals with alzheimer's disease during an activity of daily living. *Journal of Speech, Language, and Hearing Research*, 55:328–341.

Wilson, Rozanne, Elizabeth Rochon, Alex Mihailidis, and Carol Léonard. submitted. Quantitative analysis of formal caregivers' use of communication strategies while assisting individuals with moderate and severe alzheimer's disease during oral care. *Journal of Speech, Language, and Hearing Research*.

Generating Situated Assisting Utterances to Facilitate Tactile-Map Understanding: A Prototype System

Kris Lohmann, **Ole Eichhorn**, and **Timo Baumann**
Department of Informatics, University of Hamburg
Vogt-Kölln-Straße 30
22527 Hamburg, Germany
{lohmann,9eichhor,baumann}@informatik.uni-hamburg.de

Abstract

Tactile maps are important substitutes for visual maps for blind and visually impaired people and the efficiency of tactile-map reading can largely be improved by giving assisting utterances that make use of spatial language. In this paper, we elaborate earlier ideas for a system that generates such utterances and present a prototype implementation based on a semantic conceptualization of the movements that the map user performs. A worked example shows the plausibility of the solution and the output that the prototype generates given input derived from experimental data.

1 Introduction

Humans use maps in everyday scenarios. Especially for blind and visually impaired people, tactile maps are helpful accessible substitutes for visual maps (Espinosa, Ungar, Ochaita, Blades, & Spencer, 1998; Ungar, 2000). However, tactile maps are less efficient than visual maps, as they have to be read sequentially. A further problem of physical tactile maps is restricted availability. While physical tactile maps are rarely available and costly to produce, modern haptic human-computer interfaces can be used to present virtual variants of tactile maps (*virtual tactile maps*) providing a similar functionality. For example, the Sensable Phantom Omni device used in our research enables a user to feel virtual three-dimensional objects (see Figure 1). It can be thought of as a reverse robotic arm that makes virtual haptic perception possible by generating force feedback. In the context of the research discussed, these objects are virtual tactile maps. These consist of a virtual plane on which streets and potential landmarks (such as buildings) are presented as cavities.

In recent work, Habel, Kerzel, and Lohmann (2010) have suggested a multi-modal map called *Verbally Assisting Virtual-Environment Tactile Map* (VAVETaM) with the goal to enable more efficient acquisition of spatial survey (overview) knowledge for blind and visually impaired people.

VAVETaM extends the approaches towards multimodal maps (see Section 2) by generating situated spatial language. The prototype described reacts to the user's exploration movements more like a human verbally assisting a tactile map reader would do, e.g., by describing spatial relations between objects on the map. The users may explore the map freely, i.e., they choose which map objects are of interest and in which order they explore them. This demands for situated natural language generation (Roy & Reiter, 2005), which produces timely appropriate assisting utterances. Previously, the suggested system has not been implemented.

The goal of this paper is to show that the ideas of Lohmann, Kerzel, and Habel (2010) and Lohmann, Eschenbach, and Habel (2011) can be implemented in a prototype which is able to generate helpful assisting utterances; that is, to show that the language-generation components of VAVETaM are technically possible. The remainder of the paper is structured as follows: We first briefly survey some related work in Section 2, and then describe the overall structure of VAVETaM in Section 3. We then present a description of our system in Section 4 paying special attention to the input to natural language generation (Subsection 4.1) and the generation component itself (Subsection 4.2). We show the appropriateness of the approach by discussing an example input, the pro-

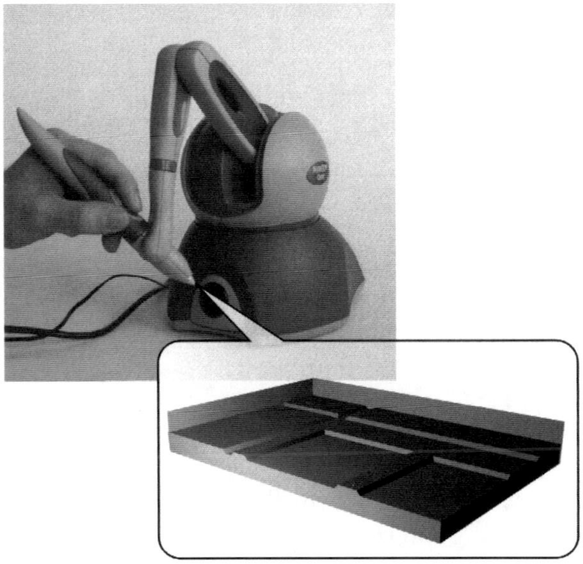

Figure 1: The Sensable Omni Haptic Device and a Visualization of a Virtual Tactile Map.

cesses performed, and the automatically generated output in Section 5 before we close with concluding remarks in Section 6.

2 Related Work

To make maps more accessible for visually impaired people by overcoming drawbacks of uni-modal tactile maps, a number of multi-modal systems that combine haptics and sound have been developed. An early system is the NOMAD system. It is based on a traditional physical tactile map, which is placed on a touch pad. The system allows for the association of sound to objects on the map (Parkes, 1988, 1994). The approach to use traditional physical tactile maps as overlays on touch pads has been used in various systems that were developed subsequently (e.g., Miele, Landau, & Gilden, 2006; Wang, Li, Hedgpeth, & Haven, 2009). Overviews of research on accessible maps for blind and visually impaired people can be found in Buzzi, Buzzi, Leporini, and Martusciello (2011) and in De Almeida (Vasconcellos) and Tsuji (2005). Other researchers have advanced the way haptic perception is realized by using more flexible human-computer-interaction systems that do not need physical tactile map overlays. For example, Zeng and Weber (2010) have proposed an audio-tactile system which is based on a large-scale braille display and De Felice, Renna, Attolico, and Distante (2007) presented the Omero system, which makes use of a virtual haptic interface similar to the interface used in our research.

Existing systems work on the basis of sounds or canned texts that are associated to objects or areas on the map. Sound playback starts when the user touches a map object or, in some systems, by clicking or tapping on it. Yet, when humans are asked to verbally assist a virtual tactile map explorer, they produce assisting utterances in which they make much more use of spatial language and give brief augmenting descriptions of the objects that are currently explored and their surroundings (Lohmann et al., 2011). Based on this, Lohmann and colleagues suggest which informational content should be included in assisting utterances for a tactile-map reading task. Among the types of information that are suggested for verbal assisting utterances is information allowing for identification of objects, e.g., by stating its name (e.g., 'This is 42nd Avenue'); information about the spatial relation of objects ('The church is above the museum'); and talking about the ends of streets that are explored ('This street is restricted to the left by the map frame').

Empirical (Wizard-of-Oz-like) research with 24 blindfolded sighted participants has concerned an audio-tactile system that makes use of assisting utterances containing the information discussed above and shown its potential. Different outcome measures, among them sketch maps and a verbal task, showed an improved knowledge acquisition with verbal assisting utterances compared to a baseline condition in which participants verbally only received information about the names of objects (Lohmann & Habel, forthcoming). Empirical research with blind and visually impaired people is ongoing. Data from the ongoing experiment with blind and visually impaired participants is used to show the function of the system in Section 5.

3 The Structure of VAVETaM

In this section we will recap the overall structure of VAVETaM as presented by Habel et al. (2010) and Lohmann et al. (2010). Figure 2 depicts the relevant parts of the structure.

The *Virtual-Environment Tactile Map* (VETM)

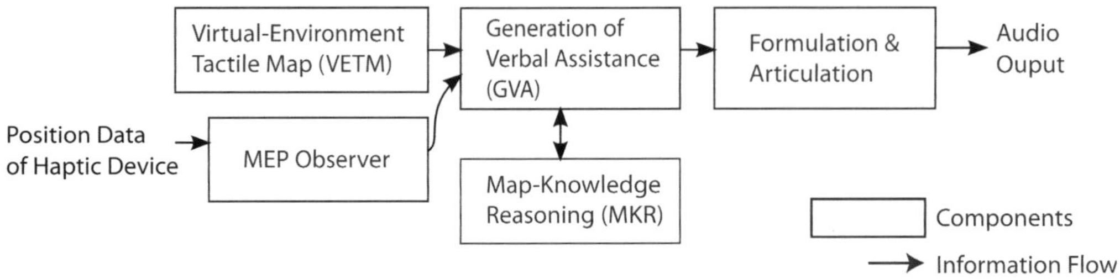

Figure 2: The Interaction of the Generation Components with Other Components of VAVETaM (modified version following Habel et al., 2010).

knowledge base forms the basis for rendering the tactile map, for analyzing movements, and for verbalizing assistive utterances forming the central knowledge component in the architecture.

Knowledge needed for natural-language generation is represented in a propositional format which is linked to knowledge needed for movement classification and for the haptic presentation of the map. The latter is stored in a spatial-geometric, coordinate-based format. The knowledge for assistance generation is represented using the Referential-Nets formalism developed by Habel (1986) and successfully used by Guhe, Habel, and Tschander (2004) for natural language generation. Knowledge for verbalization is organized by interrelated Referential Objects (RefOs), which are the potential objects of discourse. A referential object consists of an identifier for the object (an arbitrary string, for example pt3), additional associated information such as the sort of the object, and associated propositional information that can be verbalized (such as the name of the object and relations to other objects, e.g., that the object is 'left of' another object). Important sorts of objects in the map domain are potential landmarks, regions, the frame of the map, and tracks and track segments[1]. See Lohmann et al. (2011) for a discussion of the propositional layer of the VETM knowledge base.

The *Haptic Device* provides a stream of position data. This stream of data is the input to the *Map-Exploratory-Procedures Observer* (MEP Observer) component and its subcomponents which analyzes the movements the map user performs. By categorizing the movements and specifying them with identifiers of the objects currently explored by the user, a conceptualization of the user's movements is created that is suitable as input to the component dealing with assisting-utterance generation. For the case of tactile-map explorations, different circumstances affect which information shall be given via natural language in an exploration situation: (a) what kind of information is the user is trying to get (exploration category), (b) about which object the user is trying to get information, and (c) what has happened before (history).

The *Map-Knowledge Reasoning* (MKR) component serves as memory for both the MEP Observer and the GVA component by keeping track of verbal and haptic information that has been presented to the user. This component hence helps to avoid unnecessary verbal repetitions.

The *Generation of Verbal Assistance* (GVA) component, which is at the core of the prototype that we will present in Section 4, solves the central task of natural language generation. This component selects the knowledge that is suitable for verbalization in an exploration situation from the VETM knowledge base and prepares it in a way appropriate for further output. It sends *preverbal messages* (PVMs, see Levelt, 1989), propositional representations of the semantics of the planned utterance, to the *Formulation & Articulation* components for the generation of a surface structure and final utterance.

4 Description of the Prototype

In order to show how an artificial system is able to generate situated assistance in a well-formed fashion, we present a prototype implementation of the core components for natural language generation in the VAVETaM system.

[1]A track is a structure enabling locomotion, such as a street. The meaning of the term is similar to the meaning of the term 'path' introduced by Lynch (1960).

We implemented dummy components in place for the Map-Knowledge Reasoning (MKR) and MEP Observer components to allow us to test the natural language output. The *MKR Simulator* provides basic functions sufficient to avoid unnecessary repetitions of utterances by preventing production of the same message for a defined time period. An exception to this rule are those messages that are needed to identify an object on the map, such as 'This is Dorfsstraße', which are given every time the user touches an object.[2] The *MEP Simulator* generates input to the component as the MEP Observer is planned to do (see Kerzel & Habel, 2011, for a discussion of a possible technical realization).

In the following subsection, we will discuss Map-Exploratory Procedures (MEPs), which are output by the MEP Observer and form the basic input to the generation component (GVA), which we then discuss in Subsection 4.2. Finally, we present the inner workings of the Formulation & Articulation components in Subsection 4.3.

4.1 Conceptualization of the User's Movements

One of the core challenges for situated natural language generation is to timely connect the user's percepts (in the case of virtual-tactile-map exploration indicated by movements that the user performs with the device) to symbolic natural language (Roy & Reiter, 2005). The task to be solved is to have a well-specified conceptualization of exploration situations. An *exploration situation* is constituted by the kind of movements the user performs, the map objects the user wants to gain knowledge about (which constitutes the haptic focus (Lohmann et al., 2011)), and the haptic exploration and verbalization history. In the structure of the VAVETaM system, the MEP Observer fulfills the task of categorizing the user's movements and detecting objects in the haptic focus. Lohmann et al. (2011) discuss how *Map-Exploratory Procedures* (MEPs), a specialization of Exploratory Procedures, introduced as categories of general haptic interaction by Lederman and Klatzky (2009), can be used to categorize the map user's movements. MEP types are shown in Table 1.

MEP Type	Indication
trackMEP	Exploration of a track or track segment object
landmarkMEP	Exploration of a potential landmark object
regionMEP	Exploration of a region object
frameMEP	Exploration of a frame object
stopMEP	No exploration

Table 1: Map Exploratory Procedures (MEPs).

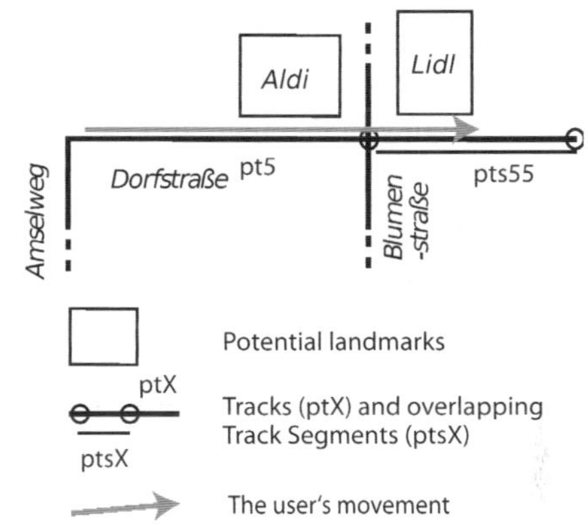

Figure 3: Visualization of a Part of a Virtual Tactile Map.

For example, a trackMEP is, straightforwardly, characterized by a track-following movement indicating that the user wants to know something about a track object. MEPs are (optionally) specified with identifier(s) that link objects on the propositional layer of the VETM knowledge base as belonging to the haptic focus of the MEP.

In this work, we extend the concept to be able to cope with multiple objects or parts of objects that can simultaneously be in the user's haptic focus. The following example illustrates overlapping haptic foci (see Figure 3). Consider the track with the name 'Dorfstraße' being represented as track object pt5 on the propositional layer of the VETM knowledge base. If the track pt5 forms a dead end, this dead end can additionally be represented as a unique track segment object (pts55). When the user explores the track pt5 from the left to the right, at a certain point, both pt5 and pts55 are in the haptic focus.

Since the user is exploring a track, the movement is characterized by a trackMEP which is specified by the objects pt5 and pts55 and either will be in the *primary haptic focus*.[3] Thus, in this case, pts55 is in

[2]User studies showed that the verbal identification is necessary to recognize the haptic objects.

[3]Notice that the decision whether in fact pt5 *or* pts55 are

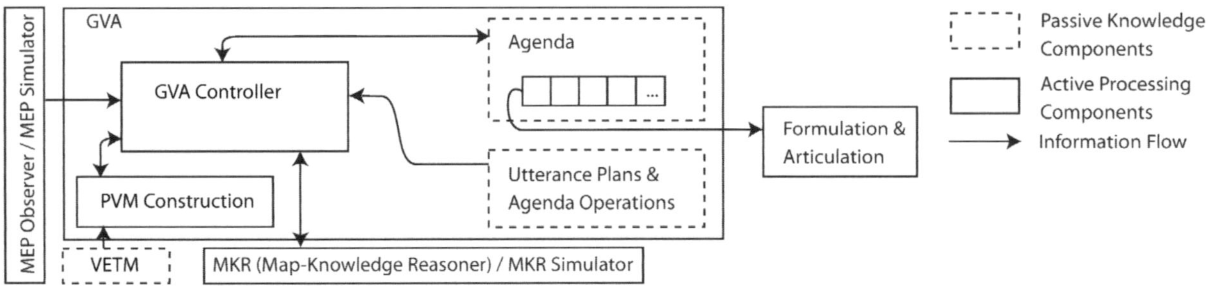

Figure 4: The Architecture of the Generation of Verbal Assistance Component.

the *secondary haptic focus*. It is reasonable to talk about both, the track and the dead end itself. As a notational convention, we denote MEPs by their type, the object in primary focus (if available), and a (possibly empty) list of objects in secondary focus. For the example above, we write trackMEP(pt5, [pts55]).

4.2 Structure of the Generation Component

The focus of our prototype is on the GVA component of the VAVETaM system that solves the *'What to say?'* task, the task of determining the content appropriate for utterance in an exploration situation (Reiter & Dale, 2000; De Smedt, Horacek, & Zock, 1996). This component interacts with different components introduced above (see Section 3): (1) it receives the conceptualization of the user's movements (MEPs and specifications) from the MEP Observer; (2) it accesses the propositional layer of the VETM knowledge base in order to retrieve information about the objects that is suitable for verbalization; (3) it interacts with the MKR component, which keeps track of the exploration and verbalization history; and (4) it then sends semantic representations in the form of preverbal messages (PVMs) to the Formulation & Articulation components.

The GVA component consists of several subcomponents which are visualized in Figure 4. The *GVA Controller* controls the execution of other processes through controlling the *Agenda*, which is an ordered list of preverbal-message representations of utterances.[4] Once the GVA component receives a (specified) MEP describing the user's movements from the MEP Observer, it looks up *Utterance Plans & Agenda Operations* that specify which information to express is suitable in the given exploration situation and where it should be placed on the Agenda. The *PVM Construction* component searches an utterance plan that allows to construct a preverbal message that contains this information. The top element of the Agenda is passed on to the Formulation & Articulation component as soon as that component has finished uttering the previous element.

In the current implementation of the GVA, utterance plans are stored as lists of potential messages and construction rules. For example, with a trackMEP, associated knowledge is stored that the object shall first be identified (by either stating the name associated to that object, e.g., 'Dorfstraße' or choosing a referring expression that allows for definite identification). Then, if available, information about geometric relations such as parallelism with other linear objects on the map is selected from the VETM knowledge base, followed by information about spatial relations with other map objects. Subsequently, the construction of a preverbal message that informs the user about the extent of the track in the haptic focus is tried, followed by information about crossings the track has. For each of these construction rules is tested whether the VETM knowledge base contains suitable information. If it does, a preverbal message is generated and added to the Agenda unless the MKR component rejects the message because this utterance is inappropriate given the exploration and verbalization history, which prevents unnecessary repetitions of information. For example, if the user has previously explored the track pt5 and already received the information that the buildings 'Lidl' and 'Aldi' (cf. Figure 3) are above the track a short time before, the articulation of this information is pre-

focussed primarily upon is up to the MEP Observer component.

[4]The term 'Agenda' is used in a similar context in the Collagen system (Rich, Sidner, & Lesh, 2001).

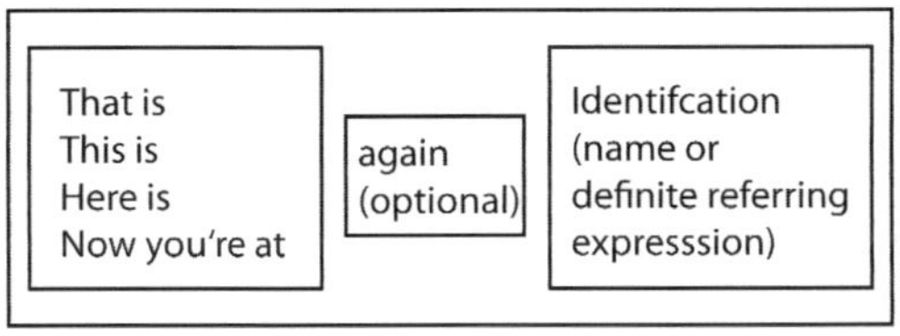

Figure 5: Literal Translation of the Template for a German Identification Message.

vented and the user is given other information (or none, if no more suitable information is available).

4.3 Formulation and Articulation

In the prototype system presented, formulation is implemented in a template-based approach (Reiter & Dale, 2000). The Formulation component uses a set of sentence templates which consist of partial lexicalizations and gaps to fill with information for the exploration situations. Additionally, a lexicon stores knowledge about natural language expressions that can be used to express spatial situations. Figure 5 shows a simple template used for the generation of identification messages.[5] Of the four utterance parts depicted in the left box, one is chosen randomly enabling some variation in the utterances. If the MKR component has marked the preverbal message as a repetition of a previously articulated utterance, a marker word is placed in the sentence (here: 'again'). Then, the sentence is completed by either selecting the name of the object in focus from the VETM knowledge base or by selecting a referring expression. The former results in utterances such as 'This is Dorfstraße'. This text is then synthesized using text-to-speech (TTS) software.

5 A Worked Example

As described, the development of the component that conceptualizes the user's movement is not yet finished. Therefore, to show the function of the implementation, we used example inputs that were derived by manually annotating screen-records from experimental data that was previously collected in Wizard-of-Oz-like experiments with blindfolded sighted, blind, and visually impaired people. In these experiments, participants received pre-recorded verbal assisting utterances that were selected by the experimenter using a custom-built software tool based on a visualization of the user's movement on a computer screen (Lohmann & Habel, forthcoming, and Section 2). Using video records of the visualizations of the user's movements, the first author manually annotated the relevant MEPs and their specifications that, in the VAVETaM structure, the MEP Observer component should output. These manually annotated MEPs form the input to test the prototype system.[6]

In order to exemplify the function of the generation system, a small part of one of the annotated inputs is detailed in this section.[7] Figure 6 visualizes a part of the movement of a visually impaired map explorer and the corresponding names and identifiers of the objects used for the specification of the MEPs in the VETM knowledge base. As the figure shows, the map explorer touches the track pt3, coming from the left. The track is explored for a while with small movements. (This position is remained for a relatively long time, maybe listening to the ongoing utterances.) Then, the map explorer proceeds to the bottom end of the track before following the track upwards. Figure 6 shows that the bottom end of the track is conceptualized as distinct track segment, track segment pts33, which is part of the track pt3.

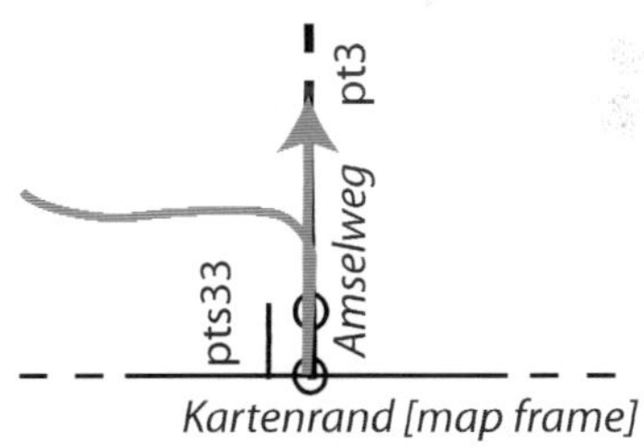

Figure 6: Example Movement a Visually Impaired Map Explorer Performed in an Ongoing Experiment.

The annotated MEPs and their specification of this small exploration movement are shown in Table 2. The GVA component and the Formulation & Articulation components generate detailed log files that in-

[5]Note that the system is implemented in German; the ordering of elements indead leads to grammatically correct German sentences.

[6]Detecting MEPs is an instance of event detection in virtual haptic environments (Kerzel & Habel, 2011), which showed its applicability for the task in an early prototype (M. Kerzel, personal communication).

[7]We also tested other annotated inputs; this example is representative of the behavior of the prototype.

Time in Seconds	Input to the GVA
...	...
33.0–54.0	trackMEP(pt3)
54.0–57.0	trackMEP(pt3, [pts33])
57.0–57.8	trackMEP(pt3)
...	...

Table 2: Manually Categorized MEPs and Specifications for the Exploration Depicted in Figure 6.

dicate which information has been selected from the VETM knowledge base, which preverbal messages (PVMs) are put onto the Agenda, and how utterances are articulated. Based on the log files, we detail the processes performed by the GVA component and the resulting verbal output in Table 3.

During the user's long first exploration movement of the track pt3 from seconds 33 to 54, which is conceptualized by trackMEP(pt3), the GVA component expresses all the information that is associated with the track pt3 in the VETM. The first message informs the user about the identity of the track by stating the identifying utterance 'This is Amselweg'. Then, the user is informed about geometric relations of this track to other tracks. In the present case, information about parallelism with the track pt4 is available in the VETM and a corresponding utterance is produced. Subsequently, the user is informed about the extent of the track, i.e., where it ends. Then, information about the intersections the track has is uttered. These are all assisting utterances that are possible given the current MEP and the knowledge base.[8]

Next, the user moves downwards resulting in the distinct track segment pts33 coming into secondary focus. All PVMs about the object in primary focus (pt3) are blocked by the MKR component, as they have just been uttered. Thus, a message that informs the user about his or her position on the track segment is formulated, resulting in a message such as 'Here, Amselweg is restricted by the map frame'. When the user leaves the track segment pt33, no further assisting utterances are given as all information associated with the track pt3 has been expressed recently.

[8]Note that the order in which information is given is fixed in the current system as explained in Subsection 4.2. Whether giving the messages in another order, which is potentially more flexible, is more helpful, has to be further evaluated.

...
33.0–54.0 s
MEP Simulator fires trackMEP(pt3)
GVA receives: trackMEP(pt3)
GVA clears agenda due to MEP change
PVM Construction is able to generate PVMs of class: Identification, Geometric_Relation, Extension, Junctions
PVMs Identification, Geometric_Relation, Extension, Junctions, are put on the Agenda (0 prohibited by Map-Knowledge Reasoner)
Formulation getting Identification PVM for the RefO pt3: the following aspects have been chosen by PVM Construction: name 'Amselweg'
Speechout: "Dies ist der Amselweg." [*"This is Amselweg."*]
Formulation getting Geometric_Relation PVM for the RefO pt3: the following aspects have been chosen by the PVM Construction: IS_PARALLEL_TO with the arguments [pt3, pt4]
Speechout: "Parallel zu ihm verläuft die Blumenstraße." [*"... which is parallel to Blumenstraße"*]
Formulation getting Extent PVM for the RefO pt3: the following aspects have been chosen by the PVM Construction: predicate HAS_UPPER_LIMIT with the arguments [pt3, ptco1]; predicate HAS_LOWER_LIMIT with the arguments [pt3, pfr3]
Speechout: "... er muendet nach oben in die Dorfstraße und endet unten am Kartenrand." [*"... it forms a corner with Dorfstraße at the top and at the bottom is restricted by the map frame."*]
Formulation getting Junctions PVM for the RefO pt3: the following aspects have been chosen by the PVM Construction: predicate IS_IN_TRACK_CONFIG with the arguments [pt3, ptco4]
Speechout: "Außerdem hat er eine Kreuzung mit der Hochstraße." [*"Furthermore, the street crosses Hochstraße."*]
54.0–57.0 s
MEP Simulator changes MEP specification to trackMEP(pt3, [pts33])
GVA receives: trackMEP(pt3, [pts33])
GVA detects secondary focus change
PVM Construction is able to generate PVMs of class: Identification
Identification-class PVM is put at the front of the Agenda (0 prohibited by Map-Knowledge Reasoner)
Formulation getting Identification PVM for the RefO pts33
...

...
Speechout: "Hier endet der Amselweg am Kartenrand." [*"Here, Amselweg is restricted by the map frame."*]
57.0–57.8 s
MEP Simulator changes MEP specification to trackMEP(pt3)
GVA receives: trackMEP(pt3)
Nothing happens, primary focus not new
...

Table 3: The Processes and Output (German and Translated) of the GVA and the Formulator.

6 Conclusion

We presented a prototype system that generates situated assisting utterances for tactile-map explorations to ease tactile map learning. The prototype is based on an earlier concept. We focussed on the GVA component in the system, which solves the 'What to say?' task of natural language generation, taking into account the situated context. We exemplified the working of the component in a testing environment based on a conceptualization of a part of a real tactile-map exploration, for which it generates plausible and timely output that is comparable to assisting utterances that were in previous research tested in Wizard-of-Oz-like experiments with blindfolded sighted people and in ongoing experiments with blind and visually impaired people. Therefore, we conclude that a generation system working in the manner described is technically possible. We also explained in detail the structure and implementation of MEPs, which are the basis for categorization of the user's movements and, with additional specification, the input to the GVA component.

More fine-grained analysis is needed to gain knowledge (1) about how much information should be given via the verbal channel to maximize efficiency, and (2) whether the system can be improved by using more flexible Utterance Plans.

7 Discussion and Outlook

One problem which became apparent in the experiments and also in preliminary tests of the fully integrated prototype system is the fact that the user's exploration movements on the map may be very quick. In these cases, the information to be delivered may already be outdated when the assistive utterance conveys this information. This is partly due to the German word order, as can be seen in Figure 5, which shows the template for identification messages.

Problems can occur in cases where an utterance is verbalized shortly before the user starts exploring another map object. In this case, the exploration situation changes during articulation. Currently, the components concerned with language generation work in a modularized sequential manner without feedback. If an utterance was sent to formulation, it cannot not be changed anymore. Hence, it can happen that assisting utterances and the user's exploration are not in all cases timely.

One possible remedy to this problem is to extend the formulation to work in an *incremental* fashion such that it explicitly handles situations in which a currently articulated utterance is outdated (e.g., an identification utterance that is no longer valid because the object to be identified has gone out of focus) and by altering it to a new utterance of similar structure (i.e., an identification utterance for a different object which just came into the haptic focus). In this case, it could *adapt* the ongoing utterance (if it is still in an early stage of production) to replace the previous identifying word (e.g., 'Amselweg') with the new word (i.e., 'Dorfstraße'). Of course, this is only possible if the articulation (text-to-speech synthesis) works in an incremental fashion (i.e., it is able to change yet unspoken parts of an ongoing utterance). Such work is currently ongoing and we plan to integrate this functionality in our future work.

Acknowledgments

The research reported in this paper has been partially supported by DFG (German Science Foundation) in IRTG 1247 'Cross-modal Interaction in Natural and Artificial Cognitive Systems' (CINACS). We thank the anonymous reviewers for their highly useful commentaries.

References

Buzzi, M. C., Buzzi, M., Leporini, B., & Martusciello, L. (2011). Making visual maps accessible to the blind. *Universal Access in Human-Computer Interaction. Users Diversity*, 271–280.

De Almeida (Vasconcellos), R. A., & Tsuji, B. (2005). Interactive mapping for people who are blind or visually impaired. In *Modern cartography series* (Vol. 4, pp. 411–431). Elsevier.

De Felice, F., Renna, F., Attolico, G., & Distante, A. (2007). A haptic/acoustic application to allow blind the access to spatial information. In *World haptics conference* (pp. 310 – 315).

De Smedt, K., Horacek, H., & Zock, M. (1996). Architectures for natural language generation: Problems and perspectives. *Trends in Natural Language Generation An Artificial Intelligence Perspective*, 17–46.

Espinosa, M. A., Ungar, S., Ochaita, E., Blades, M., & Spencer, C. (1998). Comparing methods for introducing blind and visually impaired people to unfamiliar urban environments. *Journal of Environmental Psychology*, *18*, 277 – 287.

Guhe, M., Habel, C., & Tschander, L. (2004). Incremental generation of interconnected preverbal messages. In T. Pechmann & C. Habel (Eds.), *Multidisciplinary approaches to language production* (pp. 7–52). Berlin, New York: De Gruyter.

Habel, C. (1986). *Prinzipien der Referentialität.* Berlin, Heidelberg, New York: Springer.

Habel, C., Kerzel, M., & Lohmann, K. (2010). Verbal assistance in Tactile-Map explorations: A case for visual representations and reasoning. In *Proceedings of AAAI workshop on visual representations and reasoning 2010.*

Kerzel, M., & Habel, C. (2011). Monitoring and describing events for virtual-environment tactile-map exploration. In M. F. W. A. Galton & M. Duckham (Eds.), *Proceedings of workshop on 'identifying objects, processes and events', 10th international conference on spatial information theory.* Belfast, ME.

Lederman, S., & Klatzky, R. (2009). Haptic perception: A tutorial. *Attention, Perception, & Psychophysics*, *71*(7), 1439–1459.

Levelt, W. J. M. (1989). *Speaking: From intention to articulation.* Cambridge, MA: The MIT Press.

Lohmann, K., Eschenbach, C., & Habel, C. (2011). Linking spatial haptic perception to linguistic representations: Assisting utterances for Tactile-Map explorations. In M. Egenhofer, N. Giudice, R. Moratz, & M. Worboys (Eds.), *Spatial information theory* (pp. 328–349). Berlin, Heidelberg: Springer.

Lohmann, K., & Habel, C. (forthcoming). Extended verbal assistance facilitates knowledge acquisition of virtual tactile maps. *Accepted for presentation at Spatial Cognition 2012.*

Lohmann, K., Kerzel, M., & Habel, C. (2010). Generating verbal assistance for Tactile-Map explorations. In I. van der Sluis, K. Bergmann, C. van Hooijdonk, & M. Theune (Eds.), *Proceedings of the 3rd workshop on multimodal output generation 2010.* Dublin.

Lynch, K. (1960). *The image of the city.* Cambridge, MA; London: MIT Press.

Miele, J. A., Landau, S., & Gilden, D. (2006). Talking TMAP: automated generation of audio-tactile maps using Smith-Kettlewell's TMAP software. *British Journal of Visual Impairment*, *24*(2), 93–100.

Parkes, D. (1988). "NOMAD": An audio-tactile tool for the acquisition, use and management of spatially distributed information by partially sighted and blind people. In *Proceedings of the 2nd international conference on maps and graphics for visually disabled people.* Nottingham, UK.

Parkes, D. (1994). Audio tactile systems for designing and learning complex environments as a vision impaired person: static and dynamic spatial information access. *Learning Environment Technology: Selected Papers from LETA*, *94*, 219–223.

Reiter, E., & Dale, R. (2000). *Building natural language generation systems.* Cambridge: Cambridge University Press.

Rich, C., Sidner, C. L., & Lesh, N. (2001). Collagen: applying collaborative discourse theory to human-computer interaction. *AI magazine*, *22*(4), 15–26.

Roy, D., & Reiter, E. (2005). Connecting language to the world. *Artificial Intelligence*, *167*(1-2), 1–12.

Ungar, S. (2000). Cognitive mapping without visual experience. In R. Kitchin & S. Freundschuh (Eds.), *Cognitive mapping: Past, present and future* (pp. 221–248). London: Routledge.

Wang, Z., Li, B., Hedgpeth, T., & Haven, T. (2009). Instant tactile-audio map: enabling access to digital maps for people with visual impairment. In *Proceeding of the 11th international ACM SIGACCESS conference on computers and accessibility* (pp. 43–50). Pittsburg, PA.

Zeng, L., & Weber, G. (2010). Audio-haptic browser for a geographical information system. In K. Miesenberger, W. Zagler, & A. Karschmer (Eds.), *Computers helping people with special needs, part II* (pp. 466–473).

Learning a Vector-Based Model of American Sign Language Inflecting Verbs from Motion-Capture Data

Pengfei Lu
Department of Computer Science
Graduate Center
City University of New York (CUNY)
365 Fifth Ave, New York, NY 10016
pengfei.lu@qc.cuny.edu

Matt Huenerfauth
Department of Computer Science
Queens College and Graduate Center
City University of New York (CUNY)
65-30 Kissena Blvd, Flushing, NY 11367
matt@cs.qc.cuny.edu

Abstract

American Sign Language (ASL) synthesis software can improve the accessibility of information and services for deaf individuals with low English literacy. The synthesis component of current ASL animation generation and scripting systems have limited handling of the many ASL verb signs whose movement path is inflected to indicate 3D locations in the signing space associated with discourse referents. Using motion-capture data recorded from human signers, we model how the motion-paths of verb signs vary based on the location of their subject and object. This model yields a lexicon for ASL verb signs that is parameterized on the 3D locations of the verb's arguments; such a lexicon enables more realistic and understandable ASL animations. A new model presented in this paper, based on identifying the principal movement vector of the hands, shows improvement in modeling ASL verb signs, including when trained on movement data from a different human signer.

1 Introduction

American Sign Language (ASL) is a primary means of communication for over 500,000 people in the U.S. (Mitchell et al., 2006). As a natural language that is not merely an encoding of English, ASL has a distinct syntax, word order, and lexicon. Someone can be fluent in ASL yet have significant difficulty reading English; in fact, due to various educational factors, the majority of deaf high school graduates (age 18+) in the U.S. have a fourth-grade (age 10) English reading level or lower (Traxler, 2000). This leads to accessibility challenges for deaf adults when faced with English text on computers, video captions, or other sources.

Technologies for automatically generating computer animations of ASL can make information and services accessible to deaf people with lower English literacy. While videos of sign language are feasible to produce in some contexts, animated avatars are more advantageous than video when the information content is often modified, the content is generated or translated automatically, or signers scripting a message in ASL wish to preserve anonymity. This paper focuses on ASL and producing accessible sign language animations for people who are deaf in the U.S., but many of the linguistic issues, literacy rates, and animation technologies discussed within are also applicable to other sign languages used internationally.

2 Use Of Space, Inflected Verbs

ASL signers can associate entities or concepts they are discussing with arbitrary locations in space (Liddle, 2003; Lillo-Martin, 1991; McBurney, 2002; Meier, 1990). After an entity is first mentioned, a signer may point to a 3D location in space around his/her body; to refer to this entity again, the signer (or his/her conversational partner) can point to this location. Many linguists have studied this pronominal use of space (Klima et al. 1979; Liddell, 2003; McBurney, 2002; Meier, 1990). Some argue that signers tend to pick 3D locations on a semi-circular arc floating at chest height in front of their torso (McBurney, 2002; Meier, 1990); others argue that signers pick 3D locations at different heights and distances from their body (Liddell, 2003). Regardless, there are an infinite number of locations where entities may be associated for pronominal reference; as discussed below, this also means that there are a potentially infinite number of ways for some verbs to be performed: a finite fixed lexicon for ASL is not sufficient.

While ASL verbs have a standard citation form, many can be inflected to indicate the 3D location in space at which their subject and/or object have been associated (Liddell, 2003; Neidle et al., 2000; Padden, 1988). Linguists refer to such verbs as "inflecting" (Padden, 1988), "indicating" (Liddell, 2003), or "agreeing" verbs (Cormier, 2002). We use the term "inflecting verbs" in this paper. When they appear in a sentence, their standard motion path may be modified such that the movement or orientation goes from the 3D location of their subject and toward the 3D location of their object (or more complex effects). The resulting performance is a synthesis of the verb's standard lexical motion path and the 3D locations associated with the subject and object. Because the verb sign indicates its subject and/or object, the names of the subject and object may not be otherwise expressed in the sentence. If the signer chooses to mention them in the sentence, it is legal to use the citation-form (uninflected) version of the verb, but the resulting sentences tend to appear less fluent. In prior studies, we have found that native ASL signers who view ASL animations report that those that include spatially inflected verbs and entities associated with locations in space are easier to understand (than those which lack spatial pronominal reference and lack verb inflection) (Huenerfauth and Lu, 2012).

Fig. 1 shows the ASL verb EMAIL, which inflects for its subject and object locations. Some ASL verbs do not inflect or inflect for their object's location only (Liddell, 2003; Padden, 1988). There are other categories of ASL verbs (e.g., "depicting," "locative," or "classifier") whose movements convey complex spatial information and other forms of verb inflection (e.g., for temporal aspect); these are not the focus of this paper.

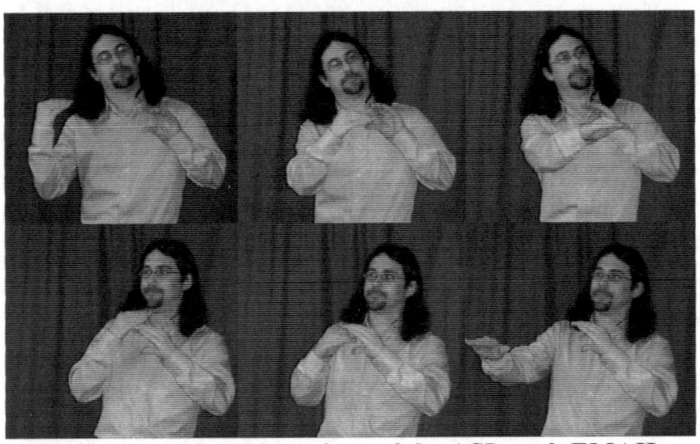

Fig. 1. Two inflected versions of the ASL verb EMAIL: (top) subject associated with location on left and object on right, (bottom) subject on right and object on left.

3 Related Work on Sign Animation

Given how the association of entities with locations in space affects how signs are performed, it is not possible to pre-store all possible combinations of all the signs the system may need. For pointing signs, inflecting verbs, and other space-affected signs, successful ASL systems must synthesize a specific instance of the sign as needed. Few sign language animation researchers have studied spatial inflection of verbs. There are two major types of ASL animation research: scripting software (Elliott et al., 2008; Traxler, 2000) or generation software (e.g., Fotinea et al., 2008; Huenerfauth, 2006; Marshall and Safar, 2005; VCom3D, 2012) as surveyed previously by (Huenerfauth and Hanson, 2009). Unfortunately, current generation and scripting systems for sign language animations typically do not make extensive use of spatial locations to represent entities under discussion, the output of these systems looks much like the animations without space use and without verb inflection that we evaluated in (Huenerfauth and Lu, 2012).

For instance, Sign Smith Studio (VCom3D, 2012), a commercially available scripting system for ASL, contains a single uninflected version of most ASL verbs in its dictionary. To produce an inflected form of a verb, a user must use an accompanying piece of software to precisely pose a character's hands to produce a verb sign; this significantly slows down the process of scripting an ASL animation. One British Sign Language animation generator (Marshall and Safar, 2005) can associate entities under discussion with a finite number of locations in space (approximately 6). Its repertoire also includes a few verbs whose subject/object are positioned at these locations. However, most of the verbs handled by their system involved relatively simple motion paths for the hands from subject to object locations, and the system did not allow for the arrangement of pronominal reference points at arbitrary locations in space.

Toro (Toro, 2004; 2005) focused on ASL inflected verbs; they analyzed the videos of human signers to note the 2D hand locations in the image for different verbs. Next, they wrote animation code for planning motion paths for the hands based on their observations. A limitation of this work is that asking humans to look for hand locations in a video and write down angles and coordinates is inexact; further, a human looked for patterns in the data – machine learning approaches were not used.

There are some sign language animation researchers who have used modeling techniques applied to human motion data. Researchers studying coarticulation for French Sign Language (LSF) animations (Segouat & Braffort, 2009) digitally analyzed the movements of human signers in video and trained mathematical models of the movements between signs, which could be used during animation synthesis. Because collecting data from human via video requires researchers to estimate movements from a 2D image, it is more accurate and efficient to use motion-capture sensors. Duarte et al. collected data via motion capture in their SignCom project for LSF (Duarte and Gibet, 2011), and they reassembled elements of the recordings to synthesize novel animations.

4 Our Prior Modeling Research

The goal of our research is to construct computational models of ASL verbs that can automate the work of human users of scripting software or be used within generation. Given the name of the verb, the location in space associated with verb's subject, and the location associated with the object, our software should access its parameterized lexicon of ASL verb signs to synthesize the specific inflected form needed for a sentence. Our technique for building these parameterized lexicon entries for each verb is data-driven: based on samples of sign language motion from human signers. Specifically, we record a list of examples of each verb for a variety of arrangements of the verb's subject and object around the signer's body. Fig. 2. shows how we identified 7 locations on an arc around the signer; we then collected examples of each verb for all possible combinations of these seven locations for subject and object. Table 1 lists the ASL verbs modeled in our prior work (Huenerfauth and Lu, 2010; Lu and Huenerfauth, 2011).

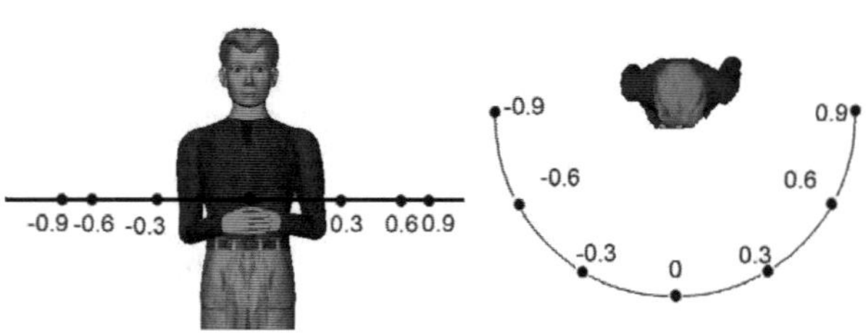

Fig. 2. Front & top view of arc positions around the signer.

Table 1: Five ASL Verbs We Have Modeled

Verb	*Inflection Type*	*Description*
ASK	Subject & Object	The signer moves an extended index finger from the "asker" (subject) to the "person being asked" (object). During the movement, the finger bends into a hooked shape. (ASL "1" to "X" handshape.)
GIVE	Subject & Object	In this two-handed version of the sign, the signer moves two hands as a pair from the "giver" (subject) toward the "recipient" (object). (Both hands have an ASL "flat-O" handshape.)
MEET	Subject & Object	Signer moves two index fingers towards each other (pointing upward) to "meet" at some point in the middle. (ASL "1" handshape.)
SCOLD	Object Only	The signer "wags" (bounces up and down while pointing) an extended index finger at the "person being scolded" (object). (ASL "1" handshape.)
TELL	Object Only	The signer moves an extended index finger from the mouth/chin toward the "person being told" (object). (ASL "1" handshape.)

For verbs inflected for both subject and object location (MEET, GIVE), our training data contained 42 examples for all non-reflexive combinations of the 7 arc positions. For verbs inflected for object location only (TELL, SCOLD, ASK), 7 examples were collected. While we focused on these five verbs as examples, we intend for our lexicon building methodology to be generalizable to other verbs and other sign languages. In our early work (Huenerfauth and Lu, 2010), we collected samples of inflected verbs by asking a native ASL signer with animation experience to produce these verbs using the Gesture Builder sign creation software (VCom3D, 2012). In later work, we collected more natural/accurate data by using motion-capture equipment to record a human signer performing a verb for various arrangements of subject/object in space (Lu and Huenerfauth, 2011).

Regardless of the data source, we extracted the hand position for each keyframe for each verb. (A keyframe is an important moment for a movement; a straight-line path can be represented merely by its beginning and end.) Thus, for a two-handed verb (e.g., GIVE) that is inflected for both subject and object, we collected 504 location values: 42 examples x 2 keyframes x 2 hands x 3 (x, y, z) values. Next, we fit third-order polynomial models for each dimension (x, y, z) of the hand position at each keyframe – parameterized on the arc locations of the verb's subject and object for that instance in the training data (Huenerfauth and Lu, 2010).

At this point, we could use the model to synthesize novel ASL verb sign instances (properly inflected for different locations of subject and object, including combinations not present in the training data) by predicting the location of the hand for each of the keyframes of a verb, given the location of the verb's subject and object on the arc. Our animation software is keyframe based, and it uses inverse kinematics and motion interpolation to synthesize a full animation from a list of hand location targets for specific keyframe times during the animation. Additional details appear in (Huenerfauth and Lu, 2010; Lu and Huenerfauth, 2011).

To evaluate our models in prior work, we conducted a variety of user-based and distance-metric-based evaluations. For instance, we showed native ASL signer participants animations of short ASL stories that contained verbs (some versions produced by our model, and some produced by a human animator) to measure whether the stories containing our modeled verbs were easily understood, as measured on comprehension questions or side-by-side subjective evaluations (Huenerfauth and Lu, 2010). No significant differences in comprehension or evaluation scores were observed in these prior studies, indicating that the ASL animations synthesized from our model had similar quality to verb signs produced by a human animator.

5 Collecting More Verb Examples

In prior work, we used motion-capture data from only a single human signer performing many inflected forms of five ASL verbs. For this paper, we asked two additional signers to perform examples of each inflected form of the five verbs. This section summarizes the collection methodology, described in detail in (Lu and Huenerfauth, 2011). During a videotaped 90-minute recording session, each native ASL signer wore a set of motion-capture sensors while performing a set of ASL verb signs, for various given arrangements of the subject and object in the signing space. We use an Intersense IS-900 motion capture system with an overhead ultrasonic speaker array and hand, head, and torso mounted sensors with directional microphones and gyroscope to record location (*x*, *y*, *z*) and orientation (*roll*, *pitch*, *yaw*) data for the hands, torso, and head of the signer during the study. We placed colored targets around the perimeter of the laboratory at precise angles, relative to where the signer was seated, corresponding to the points on the arc in Fig. 2. Fig. 4. shows how we set up the laboratory during the data collection with 10cm colored paper squares were attached to the walls; the two squares visible in Fig. 4 correspond to arc positions 0.9 and 0.6 in Fig. 2. These squares served as "targets" for the signer to use as "subject" and "object" when performing various inflected verb forms.

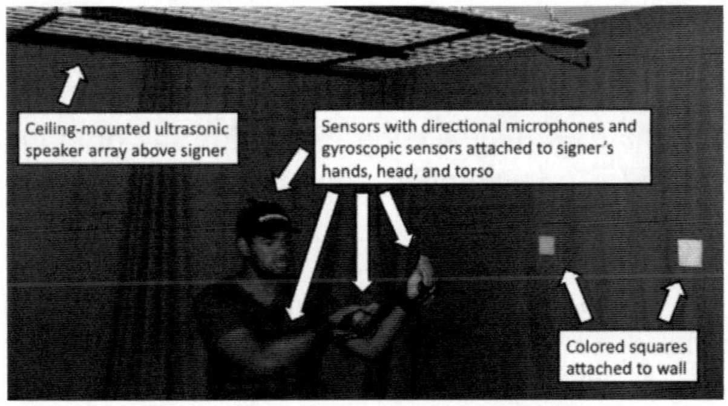

Fig. 4. This three-quarter view illustrates the layout of the laboratory during the motion capture data collection; the signer is facing a camera (off-screen to the right). Sitting behind the camera is another signer conversing with him.

Another native ASL signer sitting behind the video camera prompted the performer to produce each inflected verb form by pointing to the colored squares for the subject and the object for each of the 42 samples we wanted to record for each verb. At the beginning of the session, the signer was asked to make several large arm movements and hand claps (Fig. 5) to facilitate the later synchronization of the motion capture stream with the video data and scaling the data from the recorded human to match the body size of the VCom3D avatar.

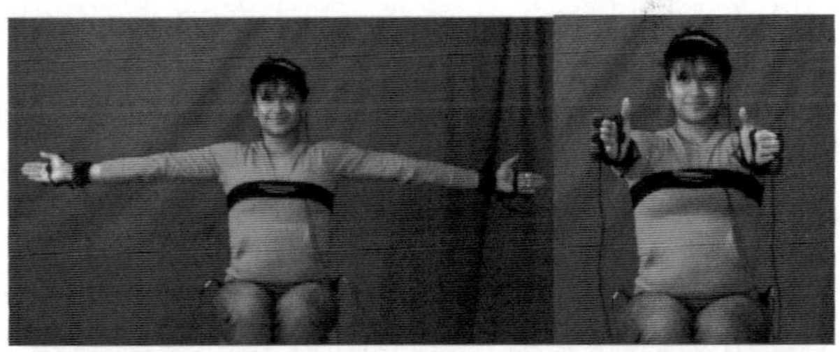

Fig. 5. Arm movements the signer was asked to perform to facilitate calibration of the collected motion capture data.

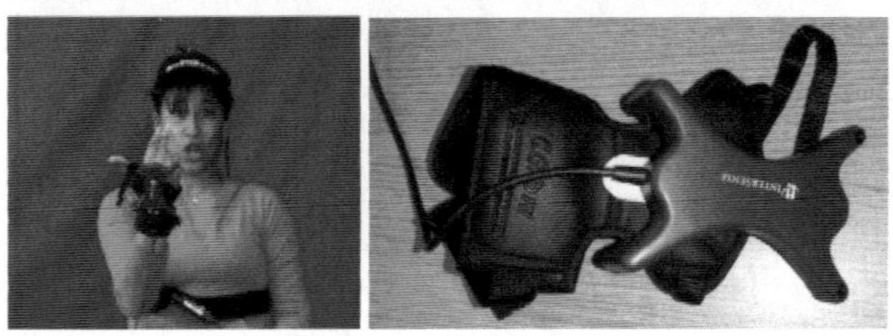

Fig. 6. The signer signed the number that corresponded to each verb example being performed (left) and a close-up view of the hand-mounted sensor used in the study (right).

Occasionally during the recording session (and whenever the signer made a mistake and needed to repeat a sign), the signer was asked to sign the sequence number of the verb example being recorded (Fig. 6); this facilitated later analysis of the video.

We needed to identify timecodes in the motion capture data stream that correspond to the beginning and ending keyframes of each verb recorded. We asked a native ASL signer to view the video after the recording session to identify the time index (video frame number) that corresponded to the start and end movement of each verb sign that we recorded. (If we had modeled signs with more complex motion paths, we might have needed more than two keyframes.) These time codes were used to extract hand location (x, y, z) data from the motion capture stream for each hand for each keyframe for each verb example that was recorded.

6 Modeling the Verb Path as a Vector

Although experimental evaluations of verb models produced in prior work based on motion-capture data from a single human signer were positive (Lu and Huenerfauth, 2011), this may not have been a realistic test. When constructing a large-scale sign language animation system, it may not be possible to gather all of the needed training examples for all of the verbs for a large lexicon from a single signer. For instance, if you wish to learn performances of a verb from examples of the inflected form of that verb that happen to appear in a corpus, then you would likely need to mix data recorded from multiple signers to produce your training data set for learning the inflected verb animation model.

The challenge of using data from multiple signers is that an ASL verb performance consists of: (1) non-meaningful/idiosyncratic variation in how different people perform a verb (or how one person performs a verb on different occasions) and (2) meaningful/essential aspects of how a verb should be performed (that should be rather invariant across different signers or different occasions). We prefer a model that captures the essential nature of the verb but not the signer-specific elements; models attuned too much to the specifics of a single human's performance may overfit to that one individual's version of the verb (or that one occasion when the signer performed). Further, while motion-capture data recorded from humans with different body proportions can be somewhat rescaled to fit the animated character's body size to be used by the sign language animation system, no "retargeting" algorithm is perfect. If signer-specific idiosyncrasies are captured in the verb animation model, then the variation in data sources used when building a large-scale sign language animation project may be apparent in its output.

Our prior modeling technique explicitly learned the starting and ending location of the hands for each instance of a verb based on a human signer's movements. However, when different signers perform a verb (e.g., GIVE with subject at arc position -0.6 and object at 0.3), they may not select exactly the same point in 3D space for their hands to start and stop. What is common across all of the variations in the performance is the *overall direction* that the hands move through the signing space. We can find empirical evidence for this intuition if we compare motion-capture data of the three different signers we recorded (section 5) performing the same ASL inflecting verbs. When we calculate Euclidean distance between different signer's starting location and their ending locations of the hands for identical verb examples, we see inter-signer variability (Fig. 7). If we instead calculate the Euclidean distance between the vector (direction and magnitude) of the hand movement from the start to the ending location between signers, we see much smaller inter-signer variability (Fig. 7). Section 7 explains the scale and formula used for the distance metrics in Fig. 7 and elsewhere in this paper.

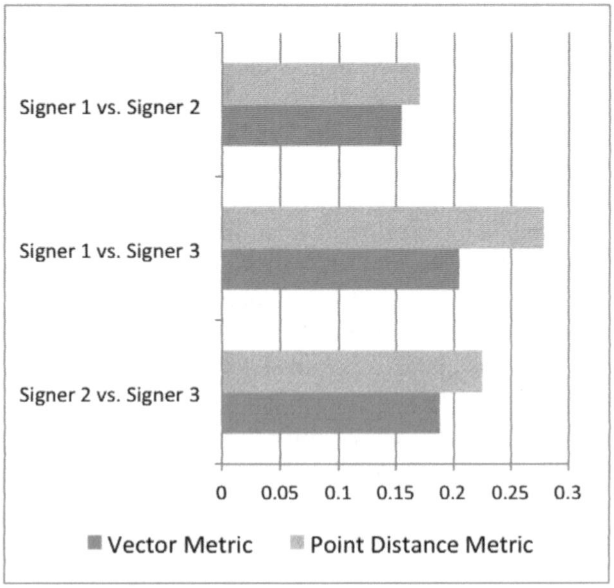

Fig. 7. Inter-signer variability in ASL verb signs, reported using a "point" or "vector" distance metric.

Using these results as intuition, we present a new model of ASL inflecting verbs in this paper, based on this "vector" approach to modeling the movement of the signer's hands through space. We assume that what is essential to a human's performance of an inflected ASL verb is the direction that the hands travel through space, not the specific starting and ending locations in space. Thus, we model each verb example as a tuple of values: the difference between the x-, the y-, and the z-axis values for the starting and ending location of the hand. (The model has three parameters for a one-handed sign and six parameters for a two-handed sign.) Using this model, we followed a similar polynomial fitting technique summarized in section 4 – except that we are now modeling a smaller number of parameters – our new "vector" model uses only three values per hand ($delta_x$, $delta_y$, $delta_z$), instead of six per hand in our prior "point" model, which represented start and end location of the hand as (x_{start}, y_{start}, z_{start}, x_{end}, y_{end}, z_{end}).

This new model can then be used to synthesize animations of ASL verb signs for given subject and object arc positions around the signer – the difference from our prior work is that these new models only represent the movement vector for the hands, not their specific starting and ending locations.

The purpose of building a model of a verb is that we wish to use it as a parameterized lexical entry in a sign language animation synthesis system; thus, we must explain how the model can be used to synthesize a novel verb example, given its input parameters (the arc position of the subject and the object of the verb). While our new vector model predicts the motion vector for the hands, this is not enough; we need starting and ending locations for the hands (an infinite number of which are possible for a given vector). Thus, we need a way to select a starting location for the hands for a specific verb instance (and then based on the vector, we would know the ending location).

We observe that, for a given verb, there are some locations in the signing space that are likely for the signer's hands to occupy and some regions that are less likely. Some motion paths through the signing space travel through high-likelihood "popular" regions of the signing space, and some, through less likely regions. Thus, we can build a Gaussian mixture model of the likelihood that a hand might occupy a specific location in the signing space during a particular ASL verb. For a given motion vector, one possible starting point in the signing space will lead to a path that travels through a maximally likely region of the signing space. Thus, we can search possible starting points for the hands for a given vector and identify an optimal path for the hands given a Gaussian mixture model of hand location likelihood.

Fig. 8 shows a (two-dimensional) illustration of our approach for selecting a starting location for the hand when synthesizing a verb. The concentric groups of ovals in the image represent the component Gaussians in the mixture model, which was fit on the data from the locations that one hand occupied during a signer's performances of a verb. Given the vector (direction and magnitude) for the hand's motion path for a verb (predicted by our model), we can systematically search the signing space for all possible starting locations for the hand – to identify the starting location that yields a path through the signing space with maximum probability (as predicted by the Gaussian model). The arrows shown in Fig. 8 represent a few possible paths for the hand given several possible starting locations, and one of these arrows travels a path through the model with maximum probability.

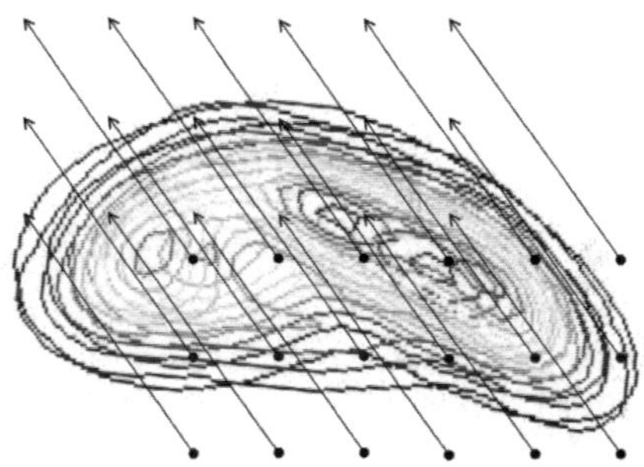

Fig. 8. This 2D diagram illustrates how the starting location for the hand can be selected that yields a path through the mixture model with maximum probability.

Specifically, for each signer, for each hand, for each verb, we used the recorded motion-capture data stream between the start-times and end-times of all of the verb examples as training data, and then we fit a 3D Gaussian mixture model for each, to represent the probability that the hand would occupy each location in the signing space during that verb. We used a model with 6 component Gaussians for modeling the signing space for each of the verbs SCOLD, GIVE, ASK, and MEET. Due to the fast movement (and thus short clips of recorded motion-capture data) for the verb TELL, we only had sufficient data to fit a 5-component

Gaussian model for the locations of the hand during this verb (TELL is a one-handed verb). When we need to synthesize a verb, then we use our vector model to predict a movement vector for the hands, and then we perform a grid search through the signing space (in the x, y, and z dimensions) to identify an optimal starting location for the hand. If run-time efficiency is a concern, optimization or estimation methods could be applied to this search.

In summary, the vector direction and magnitude of the hands are based on a model that is parameterized on: the verb, the location of the subject on an arc around the signer, and the location of the object on this arc. When a specific instance of a verb must be synthesized, a starting point for the hand is selected that maximizes the probability of the entire trajectory of the hands through space, based on a Gaussian mixture model specific to that verb (but not parameterized on any specific subject/object locations in space). All instances of the verb in the training data were used to train the mixture model, due to data sparseness considerations.

7 Distance Metric Evaluation

Because the premise of this paper is that models of ASL verbs based on a motion vector representation would do a better job of capturing the essential aspects of a verb's motion path across signers, we conducted an inter-signer cross-validation of our new model. We built separate models on the data from each of our three signers, and then we compared the resulting model's predictions for all 42 verb instances collected from the other two signers. For comparison purposes, we also trained three models (one per signer) using the "point"-based model from our prior work (Lu and Huenerfauth, 2011). Fig. 9 presents the results; the values of each bar are the average "error" for each synthesized verb example for all five ASL verbs in Table 1. The error score for a verb example is the average of four values: (1) Euclidean distance between the start location of the right hand as predicted by the model and the start location of the right hand of the human signer data being used for evaluation, (2) same for the end location for the right hand, (3) same for the start location for the left hand, and (4) same for end location for the left hand.

Fig. 9 shows that the new "vector" model has lower error scores than our older "point" model presented in prior work. To interpret the Euclidean distance value, it is useful to know that the scale of the coordinate space used for the verb model is set such that shoulder width of a signer would be 1.0. As a baseline for comparison, the average inter-signer variation (based on the values shown in Fig. 7) is also plotted in Fig. 9.

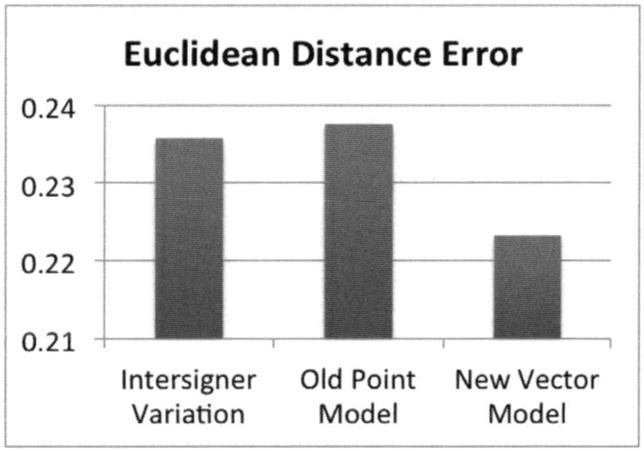

Fig. 9. Evaluation of the "Point" and "Vector" models for all five ASL verbs listed in Table 1.

Next, we wanted to compare the two models under two assumptions: (1) it may not be possible to gather a large number of examples of a verb from a single signer and (2) it may be necessary to mix data from multiple signers when assembling a training data set for a verb model. For instance, these conditions would hold if a researcher were using examples of a verb performance extracted from a multi-signer corpus to assemble a training set. Due to the limited size of most sign language corpora (and the many possible combinations of subject and object position in the signing space), a training set gathered in this manner would likely contain a relatively small number of training examples – possibly gathered from multiple signers.

To test the models under these conditions, we assembled three training data sets – using the data from our three recorded signers. Each data set included 22 examples of the performance of an ASL inflected verb for a subset of the various possible combinations of subject and object locations in the signing space – with half of the examples from one signer and half from another. After training a model on each data set, then the model was evaluated against the 42 examples of each verb performance recorded from the third signer (who was not part of the training data used for that model). This process was repeated for a total of three times (for all combinations of the data from the three signers). For comparison purposes, we also trained three models (one based on each of the three two-signer data sets) using the "point"-based model from our prior work (Lu and Huenerfauth, 2011).

Fig. 10 shows the results for two of the verbs in Table 1 (ASK and GIVE); the "vector" model has lower error scores than our older "point" model.

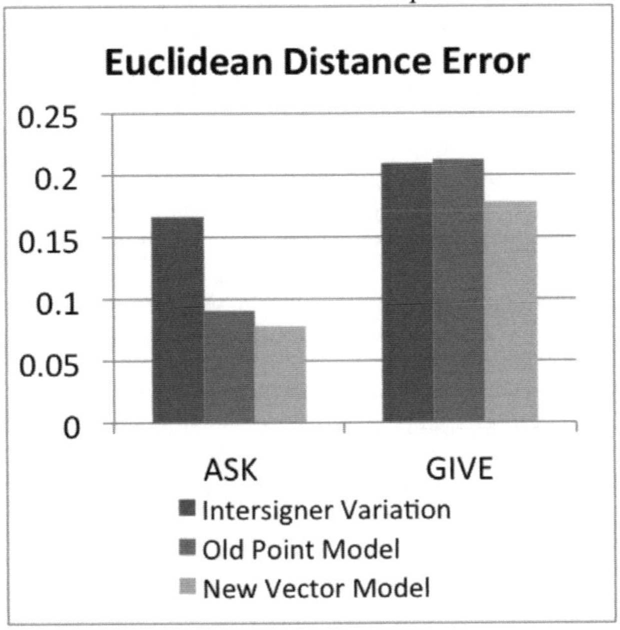

Fig. 10. Evaluation of the "Point" and "Vector" models trained on a small "mixed" data set from two signers.

Examples of animations of the ASL verbs synthesized using each of these models are on our lab website: http://latlab.cs.qc.cuny.edu/slpat2012/

8 Conclusion And Future Work

This paper presented and evaluated a new method of constructing a lexicon of ASL verb signs whose motion path depends on the location in the signing space associated with the verb's subject and object. We used motion capture data from multiple signers to evaluate whether our new models do a better job of capturing the signer-invariant and occasion-invariant aspect of an ASL inflected verb's movement, compared to our prior modeling approach. The parameterized models of ASL verb movements produced in this paper could be used to synthesize a desired verb instance for a potentially infinite number of arrangements of the subject and object of the verb in the signing space – based on the collection of a finite number of examples of a verb performance from a human signer.

Using this technique, generation software could include flexible lexicons that can be used to synthesize an infinite variety of inflecting verb instances, and scripting software could more easily enable users to include inflecting verbs in a sentence (without requiring the user to create a custom animations of a body movement for a particular inflected verb sign). While this paper demonstrates our method on five ASL verbs, this technique should be applicable to more ASL verbs, more ASL signs parameterized on spatial locations, and signs in other sign languages used internationally.

In this paper, we studied a set of ASL verbs with relatively simple motion-paths (consisting of straight line movements, which therefore only required two keyframes per verb); in future work, we may analyze verbs with more complex movements of the hands. Further, our vector models represent the magnitude (length) of the hands' motion path through space; in future work, we may explore techniques for rescaling these vector lengths. In future work, we will also use hand orientation data from our motion capture sessions to synthesize hand orientation for sign animations. We also plan to experiment with modeling how the timing of keyframes varies with subject/object positions.

Finally, we also plan on conducting a user-based evaluation study using animations synthesized by the models presented in this paper – to determine if native ASL signers who view animations containing such verbs find them to be more grammatical, understandable, and natural.

Acknowledgments

This material is based upon work supported in part by the US. National Science Foundation under award number 0746556 and award number 1065009, by The City University of New York PSC-CUNY Research Award Program, by Siemens A&D UGS PLM Software through a Go PLM Academic Grant, and by Visage Technologies AB through a free academic license for character animation software. Jonathan Lamberton assisted with the recruitment of participants and the conduct of experimental sessions. Kenya Bryant, Wesley Clarke, Kelsey Gallagher, Amanda Krieger, Giovanni Moriarty, Aaron Pagan, Jaime Penzellna, Raymond Ramirez, and Meredith Turtletaub have also assisted with data collection and contributed their ASL expertise to the project.

References

Cormier, K. 2002. Grammaticalization of Indexic Signs: How American Sign Language Expresses Numerosity. Ph.D. Dissertation, University of Texas at Austin.

Cox, S., M. Lincoln, J. Tryggvason, M. Nakisa, M. Wells, M. Tutt, S. Abbott. 2002. Tessa, a system to aid communication with deaf people. In Proceedings of Assets '02, 205-212.

Duarte, K., and Gibet, S. Presentation of the SignCom Project. In Proceedings of the First International Workshop on Sign Language Translation and Avatar Technology, Berlin, Germany, 10-11 Jan 2011.

Elliott, R., Glauert, J., Kennaway, J., Marshall, I., Safar, E. 2008. Linguistic modeling and language-processing technologies for avatar-based sign language presentation. Univ Access Inf Soc 6(4), 375-391. Berlin: Springer.

Fotinea, S.E., Efthimiou, E., Caridakis, G., Karpouzis K. 2008. A knowledge-based sign synthesis architecture. Univ Access Inf Soc 6(4):405-418. Berlin: Springer.

Huenerfauth, M. 2006. Generating American Sign Language classifier predicates for English-to-ASL machine translation, dissertation, U. of Pennsylvania.

Huenerfauth, M., Hanson, V. 2009. Sign language in the interface: access for deaf signers. In C. Stephanidis (ed.), Universal Access Handbook. NJ: Erlbaum. 38.1-38.18.

Huenerfauth, M., Zhao, L., Gu, E., Allbeck, J. 2008. Evaluation of American sign language generation by native ASL signers. ACM Trans Access Comput 1(1):1-27.

Huenerfauth, M., Lu, P. 2010. Annotating spatial reference in a motion-capture corpus of American Sign Language discourse. In Proc. LREC 2010 workshop on representation & processing of sign languages.

Huenerfauth, M., Lu, P. 2010. Modeling and synthesizing spatially inflected verbs for American sign language animations. In Proceedings of the 12th international ACM SIGACCESS conference on Computers and accessibility (ASSETS '10). ACM, New York, NY, USA, 99-106.

Huenerfauth, M, P. Lu. (2012. in press). Effect of spatial reference and verb inflection on the usability of American sign language animation. In Univ Access Inf Soc. Berlin: Springer.

Klima, E., U. Bellugi. 1979. The Signs of Language. Harvard University Press, Cambridge, MA.

Liddell, S. 2003. Grammar, Gesture, and Meaning in American Sign Language. UK: Cambridge U. Press.

Lillo-Martin, D. 1991. Universal Grammar and American Sign Language: Setting the Null Argument Parameters. Kluwer Academic Publishers, Dordrecht.

Lu, P., Huenerfauth, M. 2011. Synthesizing American Sign Language Spatially Inflected Verbs from Motion-Capture Data. Second International Workshop on Sign Language Translation and Avatar Technology (SLTAT), in conjunction with ASSETS 2011, Dundee, Scotland.

Marshall, I., E. Safar. 2005. Grammar development for sign language avatar-based synthesis. In Proc. UAHCI'05.

McBurney, S.L. 2002. Pronominal reference in signed and spoken language. In R.P. Meier, K. Cormier, D. Quinto-Pozos (eds.) Modality and Structure in Signed and Spoken Languages. UK: Cambridge U. Press, 329-369.

Meier, R. 1990. Person deixis in American sign language. In S. Fischer, P. Siple (eds.) Theoretical issues in sign language research. Chicago: University of Chicago Press, 175-190.

Mitchell, R., Young, T., Bachleda, B., & Karchmer, M. 2006. How many people use ASL in the United States? Why estimates need updating. Sign Lang Studies, 6(3):306-335.

Neidle, C., D. Kegl, D. MacLaughlin, B. Bahan, R.G. Lee. 2000. The syntax of ASL: functional categories and hierarchical structure. Cambridge: MIT Press.

Padden, C. 1988. Interaction of morphology & syntax in American Sign Language. New York: Garland Press.

Segouat, J., A. Braffort. 2009. Toward the study of sign language coarticulation: methodology proposal. In Proc. Advances in Computer-Human Interactions, 369-374.

Toro, J. 2004. Automated 3D animation system to inflect agreement verbs. Proc. 6th High Desert Linguistics Conf.

Toro, J. 2005. Automatic verb agreement in computer synthesized depictions of American Sign Language. Ph.D. dissertation, Depaul University, Chicago, IL.

Traxler, C. 2000. The Stanford achievement test, 9th edition: national norming and performance standards for deaf & hard-of-hearing students. J Deaf Stud & Deaf Educ 5(4):337-348.

VCom3D. 2012. Homepage. http://www.vcom3d.com/

Zhao, L., Kipper, K., Schuler, W., Vogler, C., Badler, N., Palmer, M. 2000. A machine translation system from English to American Sign Language. In Proc. AMTA'00, pp. 293-300.

A Hybrid System for Spanish Text Simplification

Stefan Bott
Universitat Pompeu Fabra
C/ Tanger, 122-140
Barcelona, Spain

Horacio Saggion
Universitat Pompeu Fabra
C/ Tanger, 122-140
Barcelona, Spain

David Figueroa
Asi-soft
C/ Albasanz 76
Madrid, Spain

Abstract

This paper addresses the problem of automatic text simplification. Automatic text simplifications aims at reducing the reading difficulty for people with cognitive disability, among other target groups. We describe an automatic text simplification system for Spanish which combines a rule based core module with a statistical support module that controls the application of rules in the wrong contexts. Our system is integrated in a service architecture which includes a web service and mobile applications.

1 Introduction

According to the Easy-to-Read Foundation at least 5% of the world population is functional illiterate due to disability or language deficiencies. Easy access to digital content for the intellectual disabled community or people with difficulty in language comprehension constitutes a fundamental human right (United Nations, 2007); however it is far from being a reality. Nowadays there are several methodologies that are used to make texts easy to read in such ways that they enable their reading by a target group of people. These adapted or simplified texts are currently being created manually following specific guidelines developed by organizations, such as the Asociación Facil Lectura,[1] among others. Conventional text simplification requires a heavy load of human resources, a fact that not only limits the number of simplified digital content accessible today but also makes practically impossible easy access to already available (legacy) material. This barrier is especially important in contexts where information is generated in real time – news – because it would be very expensive to manually simplify this type of "ephemeral" content.

Some people have no problem reading complicated official documents, regulations, scientific literature etc. while others find it difficult to understand short texts in popular newspapers or magazines. Even if the concept of "easy-to-read" is not universal, it is possible in a number of specific contexts to write a text that will suit the abilities of most people with literacy and comprehension problems. This easy-to-read material is generally characterized by the following features:

- The text is usually shorter than a standard text and redundant content and details which do not contribute to the general understanding of the topic are eliminated.[2] It is written in varied but fairly short sentences, with ordinary words, without too many subordinate clauses.
- Previous knowledge is not taken for granted. Backgrounds, difficult words and context are explained but in such a way that it does not disturb the flow of the text.
- Easy-to-read is always easier than standard language. There are differences of level in differ-

[1] `http://www.lecturafacil.net`

[2] Other providers, for example the Simple English Wikipedia (`http://simple.wikipedia.org`) explicitly oppose to content reduction. The writing guidelines for the Simple English Wikipedia include the lemma "Simple does not mean short".

ent texts, all depending on the target group in mind.

Access to information about culture, literature, laws, local and national policies, etc. is of paramount importance in order to take part in society, it is also a fundamental right. The United Nations (2007) "Convention on the Rights of Persons with Disabilities" (Article 21) calls on governments to make all public information services and documentation accessible for different groups of people with disabilities and to encourage the media - television, radio, newspapers and the internet - to make their services easily available to everyone. Only a few systematic efforts have been made to address this issue. Some governments or organisations for people with cognitive disability have translated documents into a language that is "easy to read", however, in most countries little has been done and organizations and people such as editors, writers, teachers and translators seldom have guidelines on how to produce texts and summaries which are easy to read and understand.

1.1 Automatic Text Simplification

Automatic text simplification is the process by which a computer transforms a text for a particular readership into an adapted version which is easier to read than the original. It is a technology which can assist in the effort of making information more accessible and at the same time reduce the cost associated with the mass production of easy texts. Our research is embedded within the broader context of the Simplext project (Saggion et al., 2011).[3] It is concerned with the development of assistive text simplification technology in Spanish and for people with cognitive disabilities. The simplification system is currently under development. Some of the components for text simplification are operational, while other parts are in a development stage. The system is integrated in a larger service hierarchy which makes it available to the users. This paper concentrates on syntactic simplification, as one specific aspect, which is a central, but not the only aspect of automatic text simplification. More concretely, we present a syntactic simplification module, which is based on a hybrid technique: The core of the system is a hand-written computational grammar which reduces syntactic complexity and the application of the rules in this grammar is controlled by a statistical support system, which acts as a filter to prevent the grammar from manipulating wrong target structures. Section 2 describes related work, in the context of which our research has been carried out. Section 3 justifies the hybrid approach we have taken and section 4 describes our syntactic simplification module, including an evaluation of the grammar and the statistical component. Finally, in section 5 we show how our simplification system is integrated in a larger architecture of applications and services.

2 Related Work

As it has happened with other NLP tasks, the first attempts to tackle the problem of text simplification were rule-based (Chandrasekar et al., 1996; Siddharthan, 2002). In the last decade the focus has been gradually shifting to more data driven approaches (Petersen and Ostendorf, 2007) and hybrid solutions. The PorSimples (Aluísio et al., 2008; Gasperin et al., 2010) project used a methodology where a parallel corpus was created and this corpus was used to train a decision process for simplification based on linguistic features. Siddharthan (2011) compares a rule-based simplification system with a simplification system based on a general purpose generator.

Some approaches have concentrated on specific constructions which are especially hard to understand for readers with disabilities (Carroll et al., 1998; Canning et al., 2000), others focused on text simplification as a help for other linguistic tasks such as the simplification of patent texts (Mille and Wanner, 2008; Bouayad-Agha et al., 2009). Recently the availability of larger parallel or quasi-parallel corpora, most notably the combination of the English and the Simple English Wikipedia, has opened up new possibilities for the use of more purely data-driven approaches. Zhu et al. (2010), for example, use a tree-based simplification model which uses techniques from statistical machine translation (SMT) with this data set.

A recent work, which is interesting because of its purely data-driven setup, is Coster and Kauchak

[3] http://www.simplext.es

(2011). They use standard software from the field of statistical machine translation (SMT) and apply these to the problem of text simplification. They complement these with a deletion component which was created for the task. They concentrate on four text simplification operations: *deletion*, *rewording* (lexical simplification), *reordering* and *insertions*. Text simplification is explicitly treated in a similar way to sentence compression. They use standard SMT software, Moses (Koehn et al., 2007) and GIZA++ (Och and Ney, 2000), and define the problem as translating from English (represented by the English Wikipedia) to Simple English (represented by the Simple English Wikipedia). The translation process can then imply any of the four mentioned operations. They compared their approach to various other systems, including a dedicated sentence compression system (Knight and Marcu, 2002) and show that their system outperforms the others when evaluated on automatic metrics which use human created reference text, including BLEU (Papineni et al., 2002). Their problem setting does, however, not include sentence splitting (as we will describe below). Another potential problem is that the metrics they use for evaluation compare to human references, but they do not necessarily reflect human acceptability or grammaticality.

Woodsend and Lapata (2011) use quasi-synchronous grammars as a more sophisticated formalism and integer programming to learn to translate from English to Simple English. This system can handle sentence splitting operations and the authors use both automatic and human evaluation and show an improvement over the results of Zhu et al. (2010) on the same data set, but they have to admit that learning from parallel bi-text is not as efficient as learning from revision histories of the Wiki-pages. Text simplification can also be seen as a type of paraphrasing problem. There are various data-driven approaches to this NLP-task (Madnani and Dorr, 2010), but they usually focus on lexical paraphrases and do not address the problem of sentence splitting, either.

Such data-driven methods are very attractive, especially because they are in principle language independent, but they do depend on a large amount of data, which are not available for the majority of languages.

3 A Hybrid Approach to Text Simplification

There are several considerations which lead us to take a hybrid approach to text simplification. First of all there is a lack of parallel data in the case of Spanish. Within our project we are preparing a corpus of Spanish news texts (from the domain of national news, international news, society and culture), consisting of 200 news text and their manually simplified versions. The manual simplification is time consuming and requires work from specially trained experts, so the resulting corpus is not very big, even if the quality is controlled and the type of data is very specific for our needs. It is also very hard to find large amounts of parallel text from other sources. In order to use data driven techniques we would require amounts of bi-text comparable to those used for statistical machine translation (SMT) and this makes it nearly impossible to approach the problem from this direction, at least for the time being.

But there are also theoretic considerations which make us believe that a rule based approach is a good starting point for automatic text simplification. We consider that there are at least four separate NLP tasks which may be combined in a text simplification setting and which may help to reduce the reading difficulty of a text. They all have a different nature and require different solutions.

- Lexical simplification: technical terms, foreign words or infrequent lexical items make a text more difficult to understand and the task consists in substituting them with counterparts which are easier to understand.

- Reduction of syntactic complexity: long sentences, subordinate structure and especially recursive subordination make a text harder to understand. The task consists in splitting long sentences in a series of shorter ones.

- Content reduction: redundant information make a text harder to read. The task consists in identifying linguistic structures which can be deleted without harming the text grammaticality and informativeness in general. This task is similar to the tasks of automatic summarization and sentence compression.

- Clarification: Explaining difficult concepts reduces the difficulty of text understanding. The task consists in identifying words which need further clarification, selecting an appropriate place for the insertion of a clarification or a definition and finding an appropriate text unit which actually clarifies the concept.

There is at least one task of the mentioned which does not fully correspond to an established machine learning paradigm in NLP, namely the reduction of syntactic complexity. Consider the example (1), an example from our corpus; (2) is the simplification which was produced by our system.

(1) Se trata de un proyecto novedoso y pionero que coordina el trabajo de seis concejalías, destacando las delegaciones municipales de Educaci6n y Seguridad ...

"This is a new and pioneering project that coordinates the work of six councillors, highlighting the municipal delegations Education and Safety ... "

(2) Se trata de un proyecto novedoso y pionero , destacando las delegaciones municipales de Educaci6n y Seguridad ...
Este proyecto coordina el trabajo de seis concejalías.

"This is a new and pioneering project, highlighting the municipal delegations Education and Safety ...
This project coordinates the work of six councillors."

What we can observe here is a split operation which identifies a relative clause, cuts it out of the matrix clause and converts it into a sentence of its own. In the process the relative pronoun is deleted and a subject phrase (*este proyecto / this project*) has been added, whose head noun is copied from the matrix clause. It is tempting to think that converting a source sentence A in a series of simplified sentences $\{b_1, \ldots, b_n\}$ is a sort of translation task, and a very trivial one. In part this is true: most words translate to a word which is identical in its form and they happen to appear largely in the same order. The difficult part of the problem is that translation is usually an operation from sentence to sentence, while here the problem setting is explicitly one in which one input unit produces several output units. This also affects word alignment: in order to find the alignment for the word *proyecto* in (1) the alignment learner has to identify the word *proyecto* in two sentences in (2). The linear distance between the two instances of this noun is considerable and the sentences in which two alignment targets occur are not even necessarily adjacent. In addition, there may be multiple occurrences of the same word in the simplified text which are not correct targets; the most apparent case are functional words, but even words which are generally infrequent may be used repeatedly in a small stretch of text if the topic requires it (in this paragraph, for example, the word *translation* occurs 4 times and the word *sentence* 5 times). While a machine can probably learn the one-to-may translations which are needed here, a non-trivial extension of the machine-translation setting is needed and the learning problem needs to be carefully reformulated. Applying standard SMT machinery does not seem to truly address the problem of syntactic simplification. In fact, some approaches to SMT try use text simplification as a pre-process for translation; for example Poornima et al. (2011) apply a sentence splitting module in order to improve translation quality.

On the other hand, other sub-task mentioned above can be treated with data driven methods. Lexical simplification requires the measurement of lexical similarity, combined with word sense disambiguation. Content reduction is very similar to extractive summarization or sentence compression and the insertion of clarifications can be broken down into three learnable steps: identification of difficult words, finding an insertion site and choosing a suitable definition for the target word.

4 Syntactic Simplification

We are developing a text simplification system which will integrate different simplification modules, such as syntactic simplification, lexical simplification (Drndarevic and Saggion, 2012) and content reduction. At the moment the most advanced module of this system is the one for syntactic simplification. In (Bott et al., 2012) we describe the functioning of the simplification grammar in more detail.

For the representation of syntactic structures we

use dependency trees. The trees are produced by the Mate-tools parser (Bohnet, 2009) and the syntactic simplification rules are developed within the MATE framework (Bohnet et al., 2000). MATE is a graph transducer which uses hand written grammars. For grammar development we used a development corpus of 282 sentences.

The grammar mainly focuses on syntactic simplification and, in particular, sentence splitting. The types of sentence splitting operations we treat at the moment are the following ones:

- Relative clauses: we distinguish between simple relative clauses which are only introduced by a bare relative pronoun (e.g. *a question which is hard to answer*) and complex relative clauses which are introduced by a preposition and a relative pronoun (e.g. *a question to which there is no answer*)
- Gerundive constructions and participle constructions (e.g. *the elections scheduled for next November*)
- Coordinations of clauses (e.g.*[the problem is difficult] and [there is probably no right answer]*) and verb phrases (e.g. *The problem [is difficult] and [has no easy solution]*).
- Coordinations of objects clauses (e.g. ... *to get close to [the fauna], [the plant life] and [the culture of this immense American jungle region]*)

We carried out a evaluation of this grammar, which is resumed in Table 1. This evaluation looked at the correctness of the output. Many of the errors were due to wrong parse trees and and the grammar produced an incorrect output because the parsed input was already faulty. In the case of relative clauses nearly 10% occurred because of this and in the case of gerundive construction 37% of the errors belonged into that category. We also found that many of the syntactic trees are ambiguous and cannot be disambiguated only on the basis of morphosyntactic information. A particular case of such ambiguity is the distinction between restrictive and non-restrictive relative clauses. Only non-restrictive clauses can be turned into separate sentences and the distinction between the two types is usually not marked by syntax in Spanish[4]. Error analysis showed us that 57.58% of all the errors related to relative clauses were due to this distinction. A further 18.18% of the error occurred because the grammar wrongly identified complement clauses as relative clauses (in part because of previous parsing errors).

For this reason, and according to our general philosophy to apply data-driven approaches whenever possible, we decided to apply a statistical filter in order to filter out cases where the applications of the simplification rules lead to incorrect results. Figure 1 shows the general architecture of the automatic simplification system, including the statistical filter. The nucleus of the system in its current state is the syntactic simplification system, implemented as a MATE grammar, which consists of various layers.

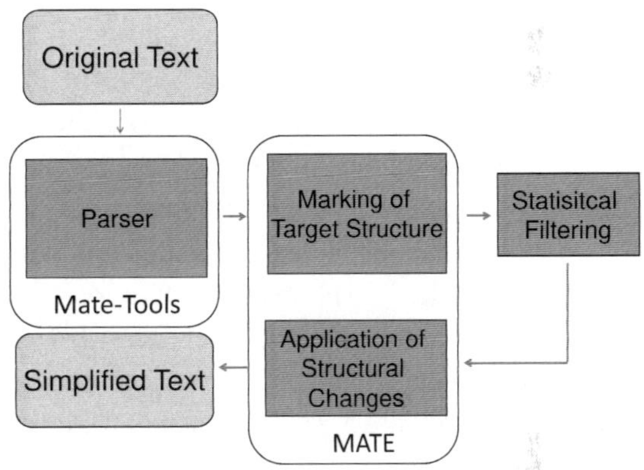

Figure 1: The architecture of the simplification system

Syntactic simplification is carried out in three steps: first a grammar looks for suitable target structures which could be simplified. Such structures are then marked with an attribute that informs subsequent levels of the grammar. After that the statistical filter applies and classifies the marked target structures according to whether they should be changed or not. In a third step the syntactic manipulations themselves are carried out. This can combine deletions, insertions and copying of syntactic nodes or subtrees.

[4]In English it is mandatory to place non-restrictive relative clauses between commas, even if many writers do not respect this rule, but in Spanish comma-placement is only a stylistic recommendation.

Operation	Precision	Recall	Frequency
Relative Clauses (all types)	39.34%	0.80%	20.65%
Gerundive Constructions	63.64%	20.59%	2.48%
Object coordination	42.03%	58.33%	7.79%
VP and clause coordination	64.81%	50%	6.09%

Table 1: Percentage of right rule application and frequency of application (percentage of sentences affected) per rule type

4.1 Statistical Filtering

Since the training of such filters requires a certain amount of hand-annotated data, so far we only implemented filters for simple and complex relative clauses. These filters are implemented as binary classifiers. For each structure which the grammar could manipulate, the classifier decides if the simplification operation should be carried out or not. In this way, restrictive relative clauses, complement clauses and other non-relative clause constructions should be retained by the filter and only non-restrictive relative clauses are allowed to pass.

For the training of the filters we hand annotated a selection of sentences which contained the relevant type of relative clauses (150 cases for simple and 116 for complex). The training examples were taken from news texts published in the on-line edition of an established Spanish newspaper. The style in which these news were written was notably different from the news texts of the corpus we are developing in within our project, in that they were much more complex and contained more cases of recursive subordination. The annotators reported that some of the sentences had to be re-read in order to fully understand them; this is not uncommon in this type of news which may contain opinion columns and in-depth comments.

In our classification framework we consider one set of contextual features arising from tokens surrounding the target structure to be classified[5] – the relative pronoun marked by the simplification identification rules. This set is composed of, among others, the position of the target structure in the sentence; the parts of speech tags of neighbour token; the depth of the target in a dependency tree; the dependency information to neighbour tokens, etc.

Linguistic intuitions such as specific constructions which, according to the Spanish grammar, could be considered as indicating that the simplification can or cannot take place. These features are for example: the presence of a definite or indefinite article; the presence of a comma in the vicinity of the pronoun; specific constructions such as *ya que* (since), *como que* (as), etc. where *que* is not relative pronoun; context where *que* is used as a comparative such as in *más....que* (more... than); contexts where *que* is introducing a subordinate complement as in *quiero que* (I want that ...); etc. While some of these features should be implemented relying on syntactic analysis we have relied for the experiments reported here on finite state approximations implementing all features in regular grammars using the GATE JAPE language (Cunningham et al., 2000; Maynard et al., 2002). For other learning tasks such as deciding for the splitting of coordinations or the separation of participle clauses we design and implement specific features based on intuitions; contextual features remain the same for all problems.

The classification framework is implemented in the GATE system, using the machine learning libraries it provides (Li et al., 2005). In particular, we have used the Support Vector Machines learning libraries (Li and Shawe-Taylor, 2003) which have given acceptable classification results in other NLP tasks. The framework allows us to run cross-validation experiments as well as training and testing.

Table 2 shows the performance of the statistical filter in isolation, i.e. the capacity of the filter alone to distinguish between good and bad target structures for simplification operations. The in-domain performance was obtained by a ten-fold cross classification of the training data. The out-of-domain evaluation was carried out over news texts from our own corpus, the same collection we used for the

[5] A 5 words window to the left and to the right.

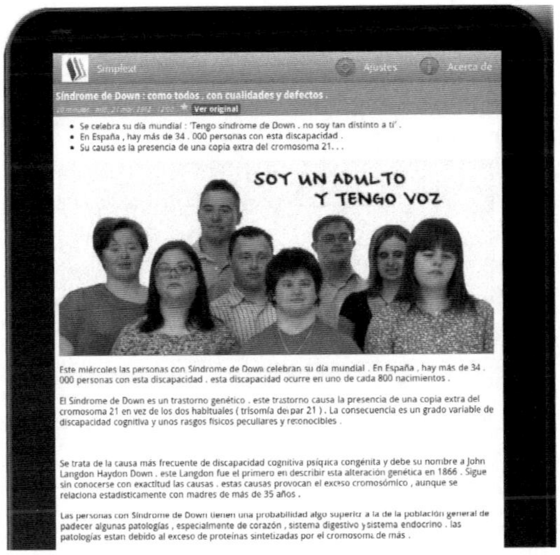

Figure 2: A simplified news text produced by the service on a tablet computer running Android

Este miércoles las personas con Sindrome de Down celebran si día mundial . En España . hay más de 34 .000 personas con esta discapacidad . esta discapacidad ocurre en uno de cada 800 nacimientos .

El Sídrome de Down es un trastorno genético . este trastorno causa la presencia de una copia extra del cromosoma 21 en vez de los dos habituales (trisomía del par 21) . La consecuencia es un grado variable de discapacidad cognitiva y unos rásgos físicos particulares y reconocibles .

Se trata de la causa más frecuente de discapacidad cognitiva psíquica congénita y debe su nombre a John Langdon Haydon Down . este Landgdon fue el primero en describir esta alteración genética en 1866 . Siegue sin conocerse con exactitud las causas . estas causas provocan el exceso cromosómico , aúnque se relaciona estadística mente con madres de más de 35 años .

Table 4: The simplified text shown in figure2

evaluation of the grammar and the combination of the grammar with the statistical filter. The performance is given here as the overall classification result. Table 3 shows the performance of the grammar with and without application of the filter.[6]

4.2 Discussion

We can observe that the statistical filters have a quite different performance when they are applied in-domain and out-of-domain (cf. Table 2), especially in the case of simple relative clauses. We attribute this to the fact that the style of the texts which we used for training is much more complicated than the texts which we find in our own corpus. The annotators commented that many relative clauses could not turned into separate sentences because of the overall complexity of the sentence. This problem seems to propagate into the performance of the combination of the grammar with the filter (cf. Table 3). The precision improves with filtering, but the recall drops even more. Again, we suspect that the filter is very restrictive because in the training data many relative clauses were not separable, due to the overall sentence complexity which is much lesser in the corpus from which the test data was taken. For the near future we plan to repeat the experiment with annotated data which is more similar to the test set. The performance in the case of complex relative clauses is much better. We attribute the difference between simple and complex relative clauses to the fact that the complex constructions cannot be confounded with other, non-relative, constructions, while in the case of the simple type this danger is considerable. The somewhat unrealistic value of 100% is a consequence of the fact that in the part of the corpus we annotated complex relative clauses were not very frequent. We took some additional cases from our corpus into consideration, evaluating more cases from the corpus where the corresponding rule was applied[7] and the value dropped to slightly over 90%.

5 Integration of the Simplification System in Applications

As we have mentioned in the introduction, our text simplification system is integrated in a larger service and application setting. Even if some modules of the system must still be integrated, we have an operative prototype which includes a mobile application and a web service.

In the context of the Simplext project two mobile applications have been developed. The first one runs on iOS (developed by Apple Inc. for its devices: Iphone, Ipad and Ipod touch), and the other one on Android (developed by Google, included in many different devices). These applications allow

[6] The results here are not fully comparable to Table 1, because in order to evaluate the filter, we did not consider parse errors, as we did in the previous evaluation.

[7] For these cases we could not calculate recall because this would have implied a more extensive annotation of all the sentences of the part of the corpus from which they were taken.

Operation	Precision	Recall	F-score
Simple Relative Clauses (in domain)	85.41%	86.77%	86.06%
Complex Relative Clauses (in domain)	70.88%	71.33%	71.10 %
Simple Relative Clauses (out of domain)	76.35%	76.35%	76.35%
Complex Relative Clauses (out of domain)	90.48%	85.71%	88.10%

Table 2: The performance of the statistical filter in isolation

Operation	Precision	Recall	F-score
Simple Relative Clauses (Grammar)	47.61%	95.24%	71.43%
Complex Relative Clauses (Grammar)	62.50%	55.56%	59.02%
Simple Relative Clauses (Grammar + Filter)	59.57%	66.67%	63.12%
Complex Relative Clauses (Grammar + Filter)	100%	55.56%	77.78%

Table 3: The performance of grammar and the statistical filter together

to read news feeds (RSS / Atom) from different sources through a proxy that provide the language simplification mechanism. The mobile applications are basically RSS/Atom feed readers, with simplification capabilities (provided by the service layer). Both applications work the same way and allow to the user functionalities as keeping a list of favourite feeds, adding and removing feeds, marking content as favourite and showing the simplified and original versions of the content. Also a web service was created, which works in a similar way for RSS and Atom feeds and allows to simplify the text portion of other publicly available websites.

Figure 2 shows a screen capture of the mobile application running in a Android tablet, displaying a simplification example of a text taken from a news website. The display text of this image is reproduced in Table 4 for better readability. The text itself is too long for us to provide a translation, but it can be seen that many sentences have been split. Also a series of minor problems can be seen, which we will resolve in the near future: The first word of a sentence is still in lower case and the head noun of the named entity *John Langdon Haydon Down* was not correctly identified.

6 Conclusions

Automatic text simplification is an Assistive Technology which help people with cognitive disabilities to gain access to textual information. In this paper we have presented a syntactic simplification module of a automatic text simplification system which is under development. We have presented arguments for the decision of using a hybrid strategy which combines a rule-based grammar with a statistical support component, we have described the implementation of this idea and have given a contrastive evaluation of the grammar with and without statistical support. The simplification system we described here is integrated in a user-oriented service architecture with mobile applications and web services. In future work we will further enhance the system and integrate new components dedicated to other simplification aspects, such as lexical simplification and content reduction.

Acknowledgements

The research described in this paper arises from a Spanish research project called Simplext: An automatic system for text simplification (`http://www.simplext.es`). Simplext is led by Technosite and partially funded by the Ministry of Industry, Tourism and Trade of the Government of Spain, by means of the National Plan of Scientific Research, Development and Technological Innovation (I+D+i), within strategic Action of Telecommunications and Information Society (Avanza Competitiveness, with file number TSI-020302-2010-84). We are grateful to fellowship RYC-2009-04291 from Programa Ramón y Cajal 2009, Ministerio de Economía y Competitividad, Secretaría de Estado de Investigación, Desarrollo e Innovación, Spain.

References

Sandra M. Aluísio, Lucia Specia, Thiago Alexandre Salgueiro Pardo, Erick Galani Maziero, and Renata Pontin de Mattos Fortes. 2008. Towards brazilian portuguese automatic text simplification systems. In *ACM Symposium on Document Engineering*, pages 240–248.

Bernd Bohnet, Andreas Langjahr, and Leo Wanner. 2000. A development environment for MTT-based sentence generators. *Revista de la Sociedad Española para el Procesamiento del Lenguaje Natural.*

Bernd Bohnet. 2009. Efficient parsing of syntactic and semantic dependency structures. In *Proceedings of the Conference on Natural Language Learning (CoNLL)*, pages 67–72, Boulder, Colorado. Association for Computational Linguistics.

Stefan Bott, Horacio Saggion, and Simon Mille. 2012. Text simplification tools for spanish. In *Proceedings of the LREC-2012*, Estambul, Turkey.

Nadjet Bouayad-Agha, Gerard Casamayor, Gabriela Ferraro, and Leo Wanner. 2009. Simplification of patent claim sentences for their paraphrasing and summarization. In *FLAIRS Conference*.

Yvonne Canning, John Tait, Jackie Archibald, and Ros Crawley. 2000. Cohesive generation of syntactically simplified newspaper text. In *TSD*, pages 145–150.

John Carroll, Guido Minnen, Yvonne Canning, Siobhan Devlin, and John Tait. 1998. Practical simplification of english newspaper text to assist aphasic readers. In *In Proc. of AAAI-98 Workshop on Integrating Artificial Intelligence and Assistive Technology*, pages 7–10.

Raman Chandrasekar, Christine Doran, and Bangalore Srinivas. 1996. Motivations and methods for text simplification. In *COLING*, pages 1041–1044.

William Coster and David Kauchak. 2011. Learning to simplify sentences using wikipedia. In *Proceedings of Text-To-Text Generation*, Portland, Oregon. Association for Computational Linguistics.

H. Cunningham, D. Maynard, and V. Tablan. 2000. JAPE: a Java Annotation Patterns Engine (Second Edition). Research Memorandum CS–00–10, Department of Computer Science, University of Sheffield, November.

Biljana Drndarevic and Horacio Saggion. 2012. Towards automatic lexical simplification in spanish: an empirical study. In *NAACL 2012 Workshop on Predicting and Improving Text Readability for Target Reader Populations*, Montreal, Canada.

Caroline Gasperin, Erick Galani Maziero, and Sandra M. Aluísio. 2010. Challenging choices for text simplification. In *PROPOR*, pages 40–50.

Kevin Knight and Daniel Marcu. 2002. Summarization beyond sentence extraction: a probabilistic approach to sentence compression. *Artif. Intell.*, 139(1):91–107, July.

Philipp Koehn, Hieu Hoang, Alexandra Birch, Chris Callison-Burch, Marcello Federico, Nicola Bertoldi, Brooke Cowan, Wade Shen, Christine Moran, Richard Zens, Chris Dyer, Ondřej Bojar, Alexandra Constantin, and Evan Herbst. 2007. Moses: open source toolkit for statistical machine translation. In *Proceedings of the 45th Annual Meeting of the ACL on Interactive Poster and Demonstration Sessions*, ACL '07, pages 177–180, Stroudsburg, PA, USA. Association for Computational Linguistics.

Y. Li and J. Shawe-Taylor. 2003. The SVM with Uneven Margins and Chinese Document Categorization. In *Proceedings of The 17th Pacific Asia Conference on Language, Information and Computation (PACLIC17)*, Singapore, Oct.

Yaoyong Li, Katalina Bontcheva, and Hamish Cunningham. 2005. Using Uneven Margins SVM and Perceptron for Information Extraction. In *Proceedings of Ninth Conference on Computational Natural Language Learning (CoNLL-2005)*.

N. Madnani and B.J. Dorr. 2010. Generating phrasal and sentential paraphrases: A survey of data-driven methods. *Computational Linguistics*, 36(3):341–387.

Diana Maynard, Valentin Tablan, Hamish Cunningham, Cristian Ursu, Horacio Saggion, Katalina Bontcheva, and Yorik Wilks. 2002. Architectural Elements of Language Engineering Robustness. *Journal of Natural Language Engineering – Special Issue on Robust Methods in Analysis of Natural Language Data*, 8(2/3):257–274.

Simon Mille and Leo Wanner. 2008. Making text resources accessible to the reader: The case of patent claims. Marrakech (Marocco), 05/2008.

F. J. Och and H. Ney. 2000. Improved statistical alignment models. pages 440–447, Hongkong, China, October.

Kishore Papineni, Salim Roukos, Todd Ward, and Wei-Jing Zhu. 2002. Bleu: a method for automatic evaluation of machine translation. In *Proceedings of the 40th Annual Meeting on Association for Computational Linguistics*, ACL '02, pages 311–318, Stroudsburg, PA, USA. Association for Computational Linguistics.

Sarah E. Petersen and Mari Ostendorf. 2007. Text simplification for language learners: a corpus analysis. In *In Proc. of Workshop on Speech and Language Technology for Education*.

C. Poornima, V. Dhanalakshmi, K.M. Anand, and KP Soman. 2011. Rule based sentence simplification for english to tamil machine translation system. *International Journal of Computer Applications*, 25(8):38–42.

H. Saggion, E. Gómez Martínez, E. Etayo, A. Anula, and L. Bourg. 2011. Text simplification in simplext. making text more accessible. *Procesamiento de Lenguaje Natural*, 47(0):341–342.

Advaith Siddharthan. 2002. An architecture for a text simplification system. In *In LREC'02: Proceedings of the Language Engineering Conference*, pages 64–71.

Advaith Siddharthan. 2011. Text simplification using typed dependencies: A comparison of the robustness of different generation strategies. In *Proceedings of the 13th European Workshop on Natural Language Generation (ENLG)*, pages 2–11, September.

United Nations. 2007. Convention on the rights of persons with disabilities. `http://www2.ohchr.org/english/law/disabilities-convention.htm`.

Kristian Woodsend and Mirella Lapata. 2011. Learning to simplify sentences with quasi-synchronous grammar and integer programming. In *Proceedings of the Conference on Empirical Methods in Natural Language Processing*, pages 409–420.

Zhemin Zhu, Delphine Bernhard, and Iryna Gurevych. 2010. A monolingual tree-based translation model for sentence simplification. In *Proceedings of The 23rd International Conference on Computational Linguistics*, pages 1353–1361, Beijing, China, Aug.

Author Index